Advance Praise for
Remember the Persecuted

"...captivating...one of those 'just can't put it down' books. While I have been deeply involved for many years in international ministry and have had many encounters with persecuted Christians around the world, this book effectively shines the spotlight on the heartbreaking situation in many nations. Likewise, this book is certainly a powerful story of how one man with vision and passion can make a difference. I pray that it will be read by multitudes."

Doug Carter, Senior Vice President
EQUIP

"In our comfortable evangelical subculture, we think persecution is a critical newspaper or TV story, or a dismissive remark from a colleague at work. We don't know real persecution because most in America have never experienced it. This book reminds us of what real persecution looks like and of what Jesus told us: that those who follow Him WILL be persecuted."

Cal Thomas, Syndicated Columnist

Remember the Persecuted

*The Story of Jim Jacobson and
Christian Freedom International*

Jim Jacobson and Melane Bower

Remember the Persecuted

New Heaven Publishing
P.O. Box 1206
Bear, DE 19701-1206
(800) 655-2859

Cover design by D3 Graphic Design

ISBN 13: 978-0-9793859-2-6
ISBN 10: 0-9793859-2-X

Remember the prisoners as if chained with them — those who are mistreated — since you yourselves are in the body also.

Hebrews 13:3

Table of Contents

Foreword

As you read this book, it is my prayer and desire that God will be glorified as you see His plan for Jim's life unfold and intersect with the lives of many of our brothers and sisters in the persecuted church.

The Bible tells us that "all things work together for good to those who love God and are called according to his purpose." It is one of the most profound and meaningful verses in God's Word. One of the key phrases in this verse is "according to *His* purpose." Too many times, we become focused on our own purpose and fail to see His. It is comforting to know, however, that God is able to see His will accomplished through us even when we lose sight of Him.

Our family was young when Jim's work with CFI began, and there were many challenges to overcome with his travel schedule. However, God provided many wonderful friends and family to support and help us while he was gone. Although there were times when Jim's extensive traveling was difficult, I knew that his calling to the persecuted church was not only for him, but for us as well. Jim and I have always taught our children that, although we could not usually travel together as a family, the ministry role that we *can* play is to allow our husband and dad to fulfill his mission to assist persecuted Christians. God's will for Jim is also His will for us.

As Jim's wife, I have been asked many times, "How do you cope with knowing that he is often in physical danger in the course of his work?" My answer is always that God has given me a deep and abiding assurance that the safest place for Jim to be is directly in the middle of His will. I have had to accept that his safety rests in God's hands, and that my worrying will not make him any safer.

God has given me many reassurances of His perfect design for my own life in many ways, but one example in particular stands out in my mind. The year was 1976, and to me, Jim was an unknown school boy living on a Michigan farm. Christian Freedom International did not even exist, and the Karen were a forgotten people, fighting a futile civil war with increasingly fewer places to escape. It was in the summer of my 13th year that a seemingly insignificant event occurred; however, in looking back, I can see the unmistakable fingerprint of God.

As a child, I loved dolls and collected them avidly. Every Christmas, I always wanted a new "collection" doll. In particular, I was fascinated with dolls that were dressed according to the culture and ethnicity of their country. In 1976, our family took an unforgettable vacation by car across the United States. One of the many places that we stopped was at the giant ocean liner, the Queen Mary, in Southern California. I had saved up a modest sum of money that I'd earned for souvenirs for the trip, and had bought quite an assortment of dolls throughout our stops. As I browsed through the gift shop aboard the Queen Mary, I was drawn to a large assortment of dolls from various countries. One doll in particular caught my eye. She was wearing a simple, white ankle-length dress with red trim. I was drawn to her, not because of the country she was from (because it didn't say), nor because of the clothes she wore. On her round wooden base were the words "Karen (Unmarried)". I was quite amazed to see a doll that shared my name, and of course, as a 13-year-old, I was struck with the fact that I, too, was unmarried. I purchased the doll, and she was displayed throughout my childhood and teenage years along with all of my other "collection" dolls. When Jim and I married in 1986, I packed them away and got them out only once in a while to show to my daughters as they grew older.

When Jim returned from his first trip to Thailand in 1997 with photographs from the refugee camps and stories of the Karen people and their plight, I noticed in the photographs that some of the girls were wearing simple white dresses with red trim. This triggered a distant memory in my mind; there was something familiar about the girls in the photos. As I thought about it, my mind went back to my old doll collection. I could hardly believe it, but I told Jim that perhaps I might have a Karen doll in the box where my dolls had been stored in the basement. I hurried downstairs and rummaged through the dolls that I had collected over the years, and there she was: a small doll, clothed in the traditional, simple white dress of a young, unmarried Karen woman. Although I'd had no idea of how intricately entwined my life would become with this people group, God Himself knew and had placed a clue in my life, even as a 13-year-old child.

As I look back, my heart is overwhelmed with praise for God's mercy and His attention to even the smallest details in our lives. As we offer ourselves to Him without reservation or preconceived notions of what we may want His will for us to be (and I confess, I have had many), He gives us more than we could ever imagine. I am a witness to this truth.

Although from our human perspective it seems unfair that we should enjoy freedom while the majority of our brothers and sisters suffer intense persecution, the Bible is clear about our responsibility to one another within the body of Christ. It tells us that "when one part of the body suffers, we all suffer." Galatians 6:10 says that we are to "do good to all, but especially to the household of faith." I pray that, as members of the body who live in freedom, this book will renew our resolve to assist, strengthen, and encourage those who are suffering for their faith today.

Karen Jacobson
April, 2008

Introduction

There are some stories that are difficult to read, and others that are difficult to write.

This story is both.

It isn't difficult because of the life of Jim Jacobson, a man who, over the course of time, has been quietly used by God to touch the lives of thousands. It's a difficult story because of the compelling—and ultimately distressing—reason why his nonprofit organization, Christian Freedom International, exists in the first place.

It exists because of an incident that took place one day in India, when two Christian workers, a reverend and a professor, were leaving a local church meeting near Jawahar Nagar. They were driving home when a group of Hindu men suddenly stopped their car, pulled them out and began to severely beat them. When police finally arrived, it was the two Christian men, not their assailants, who were taken into custody and put in jail.

The reverend, who had been beaten with the Hindu men's shoes, suffered from bruises all over his body; the professor suffered a nose fracture and spinal injury. Both were finally informed that they had been arrested because of a complaint filed against them by another local man, who claimed that they were insulting the gods by "forcibly" trying to convert Hindus. Although the Christian men were released on bail after a hearing the next day, a complaint was never registered against the Hindu men who attacked them.

It exists because of the murder of six Christians — two priests, two elderly women, and two men — who were killed by a mob of 300 armed Muslims during a midnight worship service in Ethiopia. After realizing that they couldn't enter the locked doors of the church, the mob poured gasoline around the building, then began to attack the worshipers as they came out. In addition to the six churchgoers who were killed, fifteen others suffered severe knife wounds during the vicious attack.

It exists because of the Christian family — a man, his wife, six children and father-in-law — that was arrested and jailed in Eritrea for the "crime" of praying and reading the Bible together. In the wake of a government order dictating the unlawfulness of the country's independent Protestant denominations, the family was among the first to be jailed, along with hundreds of other Protestant Christians, for the act of private worship in their own homes.

It exists because of the unspeakable violence that took place during an early morning prayer service in Yelwa, Nigeria, where armed Muslims invaded the meeting, ordered everyone in the congregation — including women and children — to lie face down on the floor, then proceeded to axe them all to death.

It exists because of the young Vietnamese man who, shortly after becoming a Christian, was summoned to a local government office and pressured to sign a document renouncing his new faith. The man was severely beaten when he refused to sign the document, and subsequently died from internal injuries.

It exists because of the house church pastor who was arrested for the "illegal business practice" of printing and distributing Christian literature and hymnals, and the government raid of two underground house churches that resulted in the arrest and imprisonment of over 80 Christians in China.

It exists because of the horrific campaign once launched against believers in Laos, where those who refused to stop praying and reading the Bible were arrested and sent to prison. During the course of their time in jail, the Christian prisoners were starved to the point of eating fungi and cockroaches. Those who did claim to renounce their faith were forced to prove it by practicing animist rituals, including animal sacrifice and drinking blood, or bowing down before idols in a local temple.

Christian Freedom International exists for one sole purpose: to come to the aid of those who are persecuted for their faith in Jesus Christ. And like many other humanitarian efforts, the mission to assist the persecuted church is without question an ongoing—and often overwhelming—one. Approximately 26,000,000 Christians were martyred for their faith during the 20th century, more than all the previous centuries combined. Incredibly, that figure doesn't even include the untold thousands who have been imprisoned, tortured, or persecuted in some other way because of their faith.

Christianity itself is, in fact, spreading at an astonishing rate in many countries, especially those in the developing world. Today in 2008, there are approximately 360 million Christians in Africa—representing just under one-half of the entire population—as opposed to 10 million Christians, which represented only 10 percent of the population in the year 1900. Twenty-five percent of Korea's population is now made up of Christians, and over 80 million Christians currently live in China, a figure that is drastically up from just one million in 1980. According to Dr. Philip Jenkins, professor of History and Religious Studies at Penn State University and author of the acclaimed book, *The Next Christendom: The Coming of Global Christianity*, a full two-thirds of all Christians on earth will live in Africa, Latin America or Asia in just 20 years' time.

But even as the world experiences such unprecedented evangelical growth, statistics also reveal that Christian persecution is on the rise. According to a recent Catholic News Agency report, approximately 200 million Christians in 60 countries around the world are currently at risk of suffering from persecution. Christian persecution has been most intense in countries such as North Korea, Iran, Somalia, Vietnam, Laos, China, India, Iraq, Bangladesh, Sudan and Burma—just to name a few.

The atrocities are spreading at a startling rate, as thousands of Christian believers continue to be harassed, abused, kidnapped, imprisoned, tortured, enslaved and martyred for their faith. Their possessions are confiscated, and their homes are raided and burned. Christian communities and churches are destroyed, and untold suffering, poverty and fear devastate scores of families each year.

Since 1998, Christian Freedom International has been on the forefront in the battle for the rights of persecuted Christians around the world. It has come to the aid of thousands of suffering men, women and children through the distribution of food, medicine, clothing, Bibles, and other basic supplies in countries where persecution is most intense. It has built hospitals, schools in refugee camps, and supports a microenterprise system that enables hundreds of Christians to provide desperately needed income for themselves through the sale of handcrafted products.

But CFI's work is not limited to the distribution of relief aid. Over the years, the organization has consistently remained active as a "voice for the voiceless" in Washington D.C., providing political advocacy for the millions of Christians who routinely suffer for their faith. It is one aspect of CFI's mission that, in large part, is what makes it unique from many other Christian nonprofits that seek to come to the aid of the persecuted church.

CFI's influence in the political arena stems entirely from the resolve of its president, Jim Jacobson, a former White House staffer who once served under the Reagan administration. It was Jim's personal experience in Washington D.C. that would prove to be unmistakable preparation for the calling he would face years later. As head of Christian Freedom International, Jim has testified before the White House, the State Department, and the United Nations regarding the deplorable conditions suffered by Christians worldwide.

But Jim is not content to simply relay stories of civil war atrocities in Burma or the militant violence unleashed against Iraqi Christians. Over the course of dozens of international trips, he has personally smuggled Bibles into China, redeemed slaves in Sudan, and delivered care packages to Christian families laboring in Pakistani brickyards, almost always at the expense of his own life and freedom. His unrelenting commitment and dedication to those enduring the bondage of persecution has become the lifeblood of Christian Freedom International.

For the rest of us who are fortunate enough to enjoy the blessing of religious freedom, this book serves as a challenge to "remember them that are in bonds" — the brothers and sisters in Christ who have never known such a blessing. Hebrews 13:3 admonishes us to "remember the prisoners as if chained with them — those who are mistreated — since you yourselves are in the body also."

Special attention should be brought to the word *remember* in this verse. On its face, the dictionary definition of the word is "to recall to the mind by an act or effort of memory." According to the *American Heritage Dictionary*, the definition of *remember* is also "to keep (someone) in mind as worthy of consideration or recognition." But in Hebrews 13:3, the word *remember* means more than just keeping something, or someone, in mind. In this Biblical context, it can more closely be thought of as the act of extending sympathy toward those who are afflicted. To remember can also mean to attend *carefully* and *constantly* to the details of something — to know it well, understand it completely, and give it its rightful due diligence — as when God commanded the Israelites to "remember" the Sabbath day, to guard it and keep it holy (Exodus 20:8).

To that end, it is not enough for us to simply have some sort of vague knowledge about the persecuted church, or even just to think of it from time to time. If we are to heed the words of Hebrews 13:3, it is of the utmost importance that we truly *remember* — to sympathize fully, and to know and understand the details surrounding the plight of persecuted Christians, just as we would know the details of a crisis involving a family member or close friend. And the more we remember, the more effectively we can support, pray for, and, like Jim Jacobson, *act* on behalf of those suffering in bonds.

Despite his active and tireless role as CFI's president, Jim Jacobson's life is unquestionably marked by the virtue of humble simplicity. Supported faithfully by his wife, Karen, their four children, and an unbreakable network of extended family, friends and co-workers, Jim's life is a testimony of the power of God's redemption, the abundant blessing of obedience, and the awesome difference that one person can truly make in the lives of so many others.

This book is not just a biography, or even a documented history of Christian Freedom International. *Remember the Persecuted* is about the people that Jim Jacobson, in the spirit of Christian compassion, has come to love so deeply: the tormented, the afflicted, and those whose lives have been taken in martyrdom because of a brave refusal to deny their Lord and Savior. The truth of their testimonies will echo throughout the pages of this book, just as surely as they will echo throughout the halls of eternity.

Melane Bower
February, 2008

The Warrior on Capitol Hill

It's heartbreaking when you think about these Karen refugees. If they didn't have an advocate, then nothing would be happening for them. I think of all the other refugees around the world who don't have advocates, who just languish for years and years in camps...the system is just so bad.

Jim Jacobson

Burma
November, 2000

NAW MU PE was eighteen years old when the bullet pierced her shoulder.

Life had already been difficult for the young girl for quite some time. Her father had died when she was thirteen, forcing her to leave school to help earn a living for the family through their rice cultivation work. Several years later, they were all forced into hiding after the Burmese army swept through the village and burned down their home.

She was seventeen when she married, and had a baby daughter soon afterwards. She and her new family continued to live with her mother and sisters, always moving from place to place out of constant fear of being discovered by the enemy.

They were preparing dinner late one afternoon when the gunfire began. As bullets pelted their home, everyone quickly realized that their hiding place had been discovered by Burmese troops. Panic stricken, the family rushed from the house.

Seconds after going outside herself, Naw Mu Pe remembered that her baby daughter was still sleeping in the house, and returned inside to grab her. As she hurried back out, she was horrified to spot her younger sister lying on the ground, dead from a bullet wound to the head. But the gunfire was still coming, closer now than before, so there was no time to stop and attend to the injured, dying or dead. Naw Mu Pe did the only thing she could to survive: she ran.

She had been running for some time when she heard her daughter moaning. After a quick inspection, the young mother discovered that her child's leg was bleeding, also from a bullet wound. But the troops weren't far behind, so Naw Mu Pe had no choice but to continue running—even when she herself was hit with a bullet to the shoulder.

After some distance, she finally felt safe enough to stop and rest. She was eventually found by her mother, who took off her skirt and tied it around the baby's leg to help control the bleeding. Although the gunfire didn't seem to be as close now, both Naw Mu Pe and her mother feared being captured by the Burmese militia. They *had* to keep running. Exhausted and bleeding, Naw Mu Pe took off her own skirt and used it as a sling to carry the baby as she and her mother ran, half naked, through the nighttime darkness of the jungle.

It was dawn when they finally reached the hiding place of some other villagers, who gave them clothes and food. But Naw Mu Pe, overwhelmed with sorrow for her dead sister and worry over her daughter's injury, was unable to eat. They had lost everything— what little property they owned, their paddies and supply of rice—when the Burmese troops confiscated them before burning their home to the ground in the sudden attack. Now they owned nothing but the clothes on their backs. She was also worried about her husband, whom she hadn't seen in hours. She would not reunite with him until the next day.

The family eventually moved on to another hiding place, where they met with resistance fighters who looked after them and treated the gunshot wound to Naw Mu Pe's shoulder and the baby's leg. Naw Mu Pe's injury would heal one month later, but her daughter, just ten months old at the time she was shot, would never be able to walk.

Naw Mu Pe knew that the memory of the attack that killed her sister and forever injured her innocent child would never be far from her mind, just as she knew that the fear and haunting sadness of life as a refugee in her own country would remain rooted in her heart. As she and her family continued to struggle for survival from their hiding place deep within the Burmese jungle, Naw Mu Pe often found herself uttering a desperate, heartbroken prayer to God: *"Why, Lord? Why do you allow this to happen to us? Why...?"*

New York, USA
September, 2006

IT WAS AN invitation that Jim Jacobson had not been expecting.

First Lady Laura Bush was hosting a roundtable discussion, The Dialogue on Burma, during the U.N. General Assembly meeting in New York, and Jim had been invited to speak about the humanitarian crisis that he had been so personally familiar with for years.

There was much to be concerned about in Burma, a country that held the record of being the world's second largest producer of opium and other illegal narcotics, while at the same time ranking among the world's ten poorest nations. A 2006 State Department report indicated that a significant number of Burmese men, women and children were being trafficked to Thailand, China, Bangladesh, Malaysia, Korea and Macau for forced labor and prostitution. The country was also plagued by monumental health problems, including drug-resistant strains of tuberculosis and malaria, and HIV/AIDS epidemics that numbered in the hundreds of thousands.

But it was the vast destruction resulting from Burma's longstanding civil war—and the Christians it affected—that had first drawn Jim Jacobson to the country over a decade earlier.

The "People of the Golden Book," or so the Karen were called, was an ethnic tribe whose history had been laced with Christianity—writings and traditional teachings about a monotheistic God called Y'wa—for centuries. According to a few legends, there had even been supposition that they were one of the lost tribes of Israel.

But there was another tale that told the story of a Golden Book, a treasure containing the truth about life which the Karen believed they once possessed. The Book had been taken by a younger, white brother to a land far across the sea, with the promise to one day return with it. As the years passed, the Karen continued to believe that their long lost Book would one day resurface.

American native Adoniram Judson would become the first Christian missionary to reach the Karen. Upon traveling to Burma in the early 1800's, one of Judson's first tasks was to translate the Bible into Burmese. He subsequently obtained a printing press and began publishing copies of the New Testament in the Burmese language.

Ko Tha Byu, a hardened criminal who'd been sold as a slave and brought to Judson by his Christian master, became the first Karen convert in 1828. As Judson shared the Gospel with Ko Tha Byu, the dawning possibility that the Bible was in fact the Karen's lost Golden Book suddenly enlightened the man. His own life was not only transformed, but the former criminal would also become known as "the Karen Apostle," the tribe's first missionary and evangelist.

His conversion had a far-reaching impact on many of the Karen people, who had already been eagerly awaiting the return of their cherished book. Just 25 years after Ko Tha Byu's conversion, nearly 12,000 Karen people would come to accept Christ as their Savior. They also took the Gospel to other tribes, including the Kachin and Chin, who were just as receptive to Christianity.

Meanwhile, as various warring kingdoms fought to conquer one another's territories, the land brewed in civil war. The Burman people, who were believed to have been the last to arrive on the scene, defeated many other dynasties and clans, eventually driving less organized tribes further into the hills. But by 1886, the region had been completely colonized by the British Empire, which eroded the structure of most of the Burmese kingdoms.

For peaceable tribes such as the Karen, British colonization meant freedom from the Burmans' repressive leadership, as well as the first chance for access to education. As opportunities continued to develop under British rule, many Karen and Karenni joined the colonial police force and army, although they were largely outnumbered by the Burman troops.

When the Japanese invasion of Burma caused the British Army to retreat to India during World War II, many Karen and Kachin left with them, only to return and help organize resistance units to fight the invaders. It was the faithful alliance of nearly 50,000 Karen soldiers that proved to be instrumental in the eventual recapture of Burma. In exchange for their loyalty, the Karen hopefully anticipated independence from the Burmans after the war — but liberation would never come. The country was eventually granted independence from the British, but despite many protests by non-Burman peoples, governmental control was returned to the Burmans in 1948. The nation once more loomed on the verge of civil war as more and more ethnic groups rose against the regime throughout the 1950's and '60's. As Burmese leadership systematically worked to cut off any and all supplies of food or funds to opposition groups and anyone who supported them, the country was thrown into abject poverty.

In 1988, a Burmese junta calling itself the State Law & Order Restoration Council (SLORC) assumed power, an organization that eventually changed its name to the State Peace and Development Council (SPDC) in 1997. It would also change the country's name to "Myanmar Naing-Ngan," meaning "Burman Country" in the Burmese language. The act was viewed by the country's other nationalities as one more deadly step in the junta's ethnic cleansing process.

As civilians were forced to surrender their land, leave their homes and relocate to army-controlled sites, many were faced with an agonizing dilemma. The lack of access to their own rice fields was causing them to forage for food wherever it could be found, or look for local day work to earn a living. But as the Army continued to use more and more villagers as a convenient source of unpaid, forced labor to work in Army camps or along the roads, survival was becoming almost impossible. It wasn't long before many people came to realize their only options: starve or flee for their lives.

Instead of obeying orders to move to relocation sites, desperate people began to hide in the jungles surrounding their farm fields, where they tried to survive by living off of hidden rice supplies around the villages and small patches of crops planted nearby. Still, access to food was minimal, and many continued to face the threat of starvation. There was also no access to medicine or medical treatment of any kind, so many people were dying from treatable diseases. As the long days turned into even longer years for thousands of displaced people in hiding, a stream of them finally began making their way to the Thailand border, only to begin new lives as refugees.

Despite increasing persecution, the Karen remained as one of the armed ethnic resistance forces that continued to fight for autonomy from the repressive junta's regime. Thousands of their own had been brutally slaughtered by the Burmans during World War II, and the wounds of history ran deep. The Burmans were just as resentful of the Karen, who in their minds had betrayed them by fighting alongside Allied forces during the war. As the unwavering conflict stretched on into the 21st century, Christianity continued to shape the Karen culture, as well as much of their struggle for political freedom. Strangely, their faith in Jesus Christ had also seemed to become a reason for their increased suffering and persecution at the hands of the SPDC. Their homes, villages and crops were burned, their women were raped, their children left orphaned, and their very existence hung in the balance, but they would not go quietly. They would forever live—and die—by the Four Principles of the Karen Revolution: there would be no surrender, the recognition of the Karen State must be completed, they would retain their own arms, and they, indeed, would decide their own political destiny. And God, many Karen Christians believed, would help deliver them from this relentless persecution.

But in spite of their determination, most of the world was largely unaware of what was happening in Burma. What the Karen needed were allies from the outside world, someone who truly cared about their plight and would intervene on their behalf.

What they needed was an advocate.

From the headquarters of Christian Freedom International in Front Royal, Virginia, Jim Jacobson had been passionately advocating for Burma's persecuted Christians since 1996. CFI had reached out its humanitarian arm to thousands of Karen and Karenni refugees over the years, providing food and medicine—sometimes personally delivered by Jim himself—for those living in jungles and refugee camps.

But CFI also provided something else—something that, in Jim's opinion, was just as important for the oppressed people of Burma. Their liberation would come only as the international community began to sit up, take notice, and take action against the brutal Burmese government. As he continued to coordinate the delivery of aid and supplies into the darkest corners of Burma, gathering firsthand stories and eyewitness accounts of atrocities from refugees themselves, Jim took what he knew to the most powerful place he could: Capitol Hill. He testified of his findings before Congress and the State Department at every available opportunity, ever hopeful to gain more support in his quest to shed light on the horrible situation.

As hundreds of children came under the care of CFI's schools and orphanages in Burma over the years, Jim also pushed for legislation allowing refugee orphans to become eligible for adoption in America. In the wake of Burma's ethnic slaughter, thousands of children had already suffered the traumatic loss of one or both of their parents. They were not only without a family, but without a state, as well: they were not recognized as Burmese citizens, those who lived in refugee camps along the Thailand border were not Thai nationals, and they weren't, according to the United Nations High Commissioner of Refugees (UNHCR) office, considered as "persons of concern." Without someone's intervention, many were doomed to live out their lives in overcrowded refugee camps.

But as indecision shuffled back and forth between the Thai government, the U.S. embassy, and the UNHCR, Jim was growing frustrated by the lack of response from the United States government. Time was of the essence for thousands of helpless children, and Jim was personally watching many orphans grow into young adults as they languished in a state of limbo.

He was not alone in the cause. The effort to eliminate adoption barriers for Karen refugees was beginning to cross political party lines, drawing support from U.S. Congressman Frank Wolfe, U.S. Senators Elizabeth Dole and Sam Brownback, and U.S. Senator Jon Corzine. Yet the White House itself remained unusually silent on the issue, even turning down Jim's request to meet with an administration official in a form letter explaining that the President was "extremely busy."

As Thailand refugee camps continued to swell with thousands of Burma's exiles, Jim also began petitioning for a law granting the asylum of Karen refugees in the United States. This, too, would become an uphill battle, brought on largely by immigration restrictions under the U.S. Patriot Act, which had been passed in the aftermath of the September 11th terrorist attacks. Jim was relentless in his Congressional pursuit to waive the Patriot Act provisions, but it would not be until May 2006 when the U.S. State Department finally announced that Karen refugees who met the eligibility requirements of the Refugee Admissions and Resettlement Program would be granted asylum in the United States.

It was a long overdue break for the Karen, although the fact remained that most of Burma's persecuted would continue to live life either on the run from its repressive military or in refugee camps, even after many others had resettled in America. To Jim, the need was still urgent, and much more work was yet to be done.

When the 61st U.N. General Assembly opened in New York in September 2006, First Lady Laura Bush decided to take advantage of the media attention to host a roundtable discussion about the ever deteriorating situation in Burma. The First Lady's Deputy Chief of Staff was on CFI's newsletter mailing list, and Jim was pleasantly surprised to be one of the roundtable invitees. Certainly, it was another valuable opportunity to speak out on behalf of Burma's persecuted Christians.

Laura Bush herself had been closely following the situation in Burma for some time, and wanted to assemble a meeting discussing ways for the U.N. Security Council to put pressure on the Burmese regime regarding the treatment of its people. The collection of other roundtable attendees was small if not varied, a total of just eight participants including Jim. All were experts in refugee, human rights, HIV/AIDS, or foreign policy issues.

To Jim, the Roundtable on Burma was instrumental in the ongoing fight for the Karen's liberation. In the ensuing days after the meeting, he had several lengthy discussions about the situation with Ellen Sauerbrey, the Assistant Secretary of State for Population, Refugees and Migration. She would become an especially cooperative ally in facilitating the resettlement process, and in helping to ensure the safety of the hundreds of unaccompanied refugee minors that would be entering the country—something that was also of great concern to Jim. His connection with Ms. Sauerbrey helped him gain a new foothold in the State Department like he'd never had before. The roundtable would also give Christian Freedom International more stature and credibility with other activists along the Burma-Thai border, who noticed coverage of the event on the BBC.

Years of long, hard work were finally beginning to make a difference for the Karen. There were still obstacles that had to be overcome, but Jim would not give up the fight. He *couldn't* give up. He would do whatever was necessary to make sure that as many of Burma's persecuted as possible would experience long-awaited independence by stepping onto American or other free soil. What was more, he could never forget about those who were left behind.

It was the sort of passion that had driven Jim for years, almost from the very moment that he had assumed the presidency of the organization that would become Christian Freedom International. His determination to turn the tides of religious persecution through the political arena would evolve as he traveled across the globe, praying with—and for—the sick and the imprisoned, bringing Bibles to the oppressed, and food to the most destitute of humanity. His advocacy work on behalf of Burma's persecuted Christians was not his first battle on Capitol Hill, nor would it certainly be his last.

There wasn't anything else he'd rather be doing, and yet there was a time when Jim never would have imagined how entrenched his life would become in the plight of so many Christians who so desperately needed help. But the truth was that, as persecution continued to worsen throughout the world, God had patiently raised up a servant to intercede for His afflicted saints...even when Jim Jacobson wasn't paying attention.

The God of Second Chances

It's "the heart of the thumb," Marlette, Michigan. It's a small farming community, and not much has changed in the 40 years since I was born there.

Dairy farming is what most people do to make a living there. My father was a farmer, and his grandfather came over from Denmark and was able to buy a small farm. It was passed on to my dad, and his dad died when he was 4 or 5 years old. My dad was raised by his mother, and they pretty much tended the farm by themselves, so he had to work hard from an early point in life.

It was small by modern-day dairy standards, but I think at one time he was milking about 100 cows, as I remember. It was a Grade A dairy farm, which means that the milk that was sold went for drinking. I just remember that he had to keep the farm very clean, very organized, and it was inspected often to make sure it maintained a certain standard.

Jim Jacobson

IT WAS AN eventful year in American history.

John Glenn, one of the first seven astronauts in NASA's space program, would go on to become the first American to orbit the earth. There was the Cuban missile crisis, the intense debate over prayer in public schools, and the launching of Telstar 1, the first communications satellite that would be used to transmit live transatlantic telecasts between the United States and Britain. It was the year when Johnny Carson assumed the role as host of "The Tonight Show," and when Hollywood actress Marilyn Monroe, in the solitude of her California home, quietly slipped into a coma and died, amid scandalous rumors of an alleged affair with President John F. Kennedy.

The year was 1962, and from their corner of the world in rural Michigan, Evelyn and James Jacobson welcomed the birth of their son, James Jr., on July 31.

He'd been born in the sort of town where farming coursed through the veins of many of its inhabitants, including his own father. James Sr. himself had been born and raised in Marlette, and had grown up on the farm he'd inherited. He was a diligent, hardworking man, but like many other farmers, struggled with the never-ending burden of financial instability.

Jim was five years old when his parents decided to leave Marlette. It was becoming increasingly difficult for the family to survive on such a meager income, and Evelyn was fed up with all of the accidents that were occurring on the farm. Both Jim and his older sister had already faced close calls after being run over by the tractor on separate incidents, and even Jim Sr. almost died after narrowly escaping his own accident with the tractor.

The Jacobsons moved to Saginaw, Michigan, where Jim Sr. took an assembly-line job at General Motors. It was a stable income, but for a man who'd spent his entire life working outdoors, the factory was not somewhere he wanted to be. The family would live in Saginaw for only a year before returning to a rural setting, this time in North Branch, Michigan. They purchased a few acres of land, enough for Jim Sr. to set up a hobby farm with 60 sheep and several beef cows. He would spend the ensuing years working various odd jobs, doing whatever was necessary to provide for the family.

Jim Sr. may have been the breadwinner, but Evelyn was the spiritual head of the Jacobson household. She'd been a Christian all her life, and made certain that her own children were exposed to Christianity from an early age. They read the Bible together faithfully, and Jim and his two older sisters, Karen and Kathy, attended a small nondenominational church with their mother every Sunday morning.

Evelyn's outspokenness about her faith was a stark contrast to Jim Sr.'s private mannerism about all things Christian. He'd been raised as a Lutheran, but never quite saw the need to wear his religion on his sleeve. Unlike Evelyn, who talked with her children constantly about spiritual matters, Jim rarely held such a conversation with his father.

Jim embraced Christianity nevertheless, and his own faith would become a springboard for the compassion in his heart that intensified as he grew older. As a child, he'd always expressed deep empathy for others, taking pity on the elderly and the sick that he would visit with his mother, or defending the kid on the school bus that was the object of a bully's unwanted attention. Somehow, Jim knew that he wanted to use his life to help others, and he wanted to do it through the church.

But options seemed limited in rural Michigan, especially considering the farming life he'd been born into. Jim assumed that, like his father, he was destined for a life of hard labor in farming, factory or carpentry work, and there was no discussion within the Jacobson family about anything outside the realm of those career choices. But deep down, Jim knew that his heart's desire was to travel the world.

His pastor, Vincent Godfrey, would become a key source of inspiration in keeping his dream alive. A devout Christian who'd served in World War II, Vincent had done some traveling of his own. He spoke often about the dire need for the Gospel in places like India and China, and frequently invited missionaries to speak to the congregation about their experiences in other parts of the world.

Vincent and his wife, Jean, who had no children of their own, soon became special mentors to the Jacobson children. Jim was especially fascinated by their stories of faraway lands, and it only confirmed his longing to see such things for himself. Through his relationship with the Godfreys, he was becoming exposed to a variety of things he never would have imagined learning about.

In time, they would also teach Jim about the importance of serving a God who never abandons His own.

AS HE GREW into adolescence, Jim was developing a strong work ethic for himself. He helped around the farm in whatever ways he could: cleaning the barn, cutting the grass, tending sheep, or planting shrubbery. At a time when jobs were scarce and the family sorely needed income, he helped his father clean stockyards, shoveling heavy piles of cow manure into wheelbar-

rows until 1:00 or 2:00 in the morning. In his own efforts to make extra money, Jim even ran a trapline,
walking five miles each day to catch muskrat, fox, and
mink. It was a small but profitable venture, especially
during Michigan's long, hard winters.

He also had a growing interest in politics, which
was another frequent topic of conversation in the Jacobson household. As a young child, he'd stood in line for
hours with his family to watch Richard Nixon's motor-
cade drive through the local streets during his campaign tour. As he watched Nixon emerge from his car,
waving to the crowds of people nearby, Jim thought
about how he would like to go to Washington D.C. and
work for a president someday. He had no idea how to
do it, or whether it was even possible, but even at such
an early age, it was an impression that would stay in his
mind for many years to come.

As a teenager, Jim began to act on his fascination
with politics. He read the newspaper regularly in an
effort to stay informed about world events, and even
volunteered for candidates running for state or local
offices, doing whatever he could to help with their
campaigns. His political aspirations never waned, but
there was one roadblock in his way: he was barely getting by in his schoolwork.

It wasn't because he was struggling with biology or
algebra, or any of his subjects, for that matter. By the
time he was in his mid teens, Jim had fallen into a state
of rebellion that quickly became the driving force in his
life. He was constantly goofing off, becoming the cul-
prit in a series of practical jokes that often landed him —
and many of his carousing friends — into trouble. Although he enjoyed running track on North Branch High
School's cross-country team, even receiving a school

letter for his participation, Jim had adopted an "I-Don't-Care" attitude when it came to just about everything else in life. It was the sort of behavior that had earned him a reputation among his peers as the classmate who would be "the least likely to succeed."

To make matters worse, he had turned away from the Christian faith of his childhood. He'd been baptized in a country stream next to the church at the tender age of eight, and had attended weekly services with his mother for years. Now, as a teenager bent on asserting some independence, Jim had had his fill of Christianity and all that it entailed.

The fact that her only son was getting away from God was not lost on Evelyn Jacobson. In one of the greatest financial sacrifices she would ever make, she removed Jim from North Branch High and enrolled him in a small, private Christian school, the North Branch Wesleyan Academy.

It was a change that would have the opposite effect of what Evelyn had been hoping for. Jim was now in an environment where Christians surrounded him on all sides, at a time when he simply was no longer open to religion. His rebellious, downward spiral would continue in a haze of good times and hard partying, until one fateful night began to turn the tides of his life.

The car was traveling at over 110 miles an hour as he sped past the stop sign, crashing into another car and then a telephone pole. Jim had been drinking before carelessly slipping behind the wheel of his vehicle, a friend in tow, before they sped off down the road. Now, other people had been injured, and all because of his own recklessness.

Furious with his son, Jim Sr. forced him to pay a visit to the hospital. It was a sobering experience, as

26

Jim witnessed for himself the damage he'd caused to the elderly couple whose car had been hit in the collision. He and his friend were also lucky to be alive, and he knew that the accident could have been much more tragic. For some reason, God had decided to spare his life.

But the incident would not be without its repercussions. He was expelled from the academy, and eventually, Jim began to realize that his life was at a crossroads. He could either continue down the path of destruction he had been following, or he could straighten out his life and make it count for something.

He chose to straighten out his life. While attending a church youth meeting shortly after high school graduation, he made another decision: he would rededicate his life to God. He would go wherever God wanted Him to go, and he would do whatever God had for him to do. For as long as he lived, Jim Jacobson was determined to follow the One who had so patiently given him a second chance in life.

IT WAS TIME for a new beginning, and it would start outside the borders of Michigan.

By the fall of 1981, Jim had enrolled in a Bible school in Dublin, New Hampshire. The decision drew strong opposition from his father, who simply couldn't understand why someone would go to school to study the Bible, when it just as easily could be studied in the privacy of one's own home. For Jim, however, the move was a logical one. The school came highly recommended by his pastor, Vincent Godfrey, and Jim was determined to serve God in some full-time capacity, although he didn't yet know how he would do it. Bible school was a place where he could study, draw closer to

God, and become grounded in his renewed faith before choosing a career path for his life.

The school was small, with an enrollment of just 30 students. It was a strict, old-fashioned environment, where many boys, including Jim, earned their tuition by cutting the firewood that heated their dormitory. His roommate was a boy named Bob Sweet, whose younger sister, Karen, also attended the school. The Sweets hailed from a family of devout Christians — so devout, in fact, that Jim candidly referred to them as the "religious Brady Bunch."

Ironically, it was Karen Sweet's seasoned faith in Christ that drew Jim into a curious attraction to the young girl. He listened as she gave her testimony at a church service near the school one evening, amazed by the strength of her conviction and the vibrancy of her relationship with a God that he himself was only just beginning to know again.

Karen Sweet was attending Bible school in her own quest to discover God's will for her life. She'd grown up under the blessing of a strong Christian heritage, passed on by two loving parents who had diligently trained all five of their children in the nurture and admonition of the Lord from the moment they were born. Her father, Bob Sweet, had a background in teaching, eventually becoming a book salesman. Despite their middle-class income, somehow the Sweets always managed to send their children to Christian schools.

While Karen was still in high school, her father decided to run for Congress in New Hampshire. He lost the election, but subsequently managed to land a job at the Department of Education in Washington D.C. To accommodate his new position, the family moved to Fairfax, Virginia in the summer of 1981. By the fall of that year, however, Karen had returned to New Hampshire to attend Bible school. She was grateful for the abundant blessings God had bestowed on her, and like Jim, wanted to use her schooling to help determine His will for the rest of her life, whatever that might be.

As it turned out, Karen was just as impressed with Jim as he was with her. He was a young man who seemed to be on fire for the Lord, always sharing his faith with anyone who would listen. For Karen, a potential suitor had to have the same commitment to a relationship with God as she did, something that Jim certainly seemed to have. And as they got to know each other, Jim and Karen found that they agreed on many political issues, as well, something that was also important to both of them.

It was an attraction that seemed to be taking on a life of its own, but after just six months in Bible school, Jim was ready to move on. His time in New Hampshire had been instrumental in helping to solidify his faith, but he was anxious to get started with his college education. He enrolled in the University of Michigan, while Karen stayed in New England to continue her Bible school studies. Neither of them realized that it was the beginning of a long distance relationship that would only be strengthened by the test of time.

COLLEGE WAS AN experience that brought about a new set of opportunities and challenges for Jim. His decision to continue with school was another point of conflict with his father, who thought that his time would have been better spent learning a trade or gaining practical work experience in a factory. But Jim remained determined—he was going to college, no matter what.

Although tuition at the University of Michigan was reasonably affordable, Jim still faced the dilemma of having to pay his own way through school. He took advantage of any and all opportunities he could find to foot the bill of a higher education, working a variety of jobs from construction to assembly line, even working at a home for emotionally disturbed children.

Jim worked hard, studied hard, and found that he liked everything about college life. He was outspoken in his classes, especially when the subject turned to some humanistic idea that usually sought to discredit Christianity. On one occasion during a biology class when the professor asked several hundred students whether anyone believed in Creation, Jim was the only one in the vast auditorium who unashamedly rose from his seat.

He had a small circle of Christian friends that he would often meet for lunch, or to attend Bible studies or prayer meetings with after class. He was also involved in many church activities, especially the youth ministry. He became a Sunday School teacher, and was even asked to deliver a sermon on more than one occasion. As more and more people encouraged Jim about his teaching ability, he eventually made the switch from business to an education major.

Although work, studies, and church were already keeping him busy, Jim also started a chapter of the Young Republicans, the oldest political youth organization in the United States. He volunteered for various candidates who were running for state office, doing everything from poll work, petition initiatives, stuffing envelopes, and even door to door campaigning. It was a tumultuous time in history, both at home and abroad, and the more he learned about socialism, communism, and the history of Western civilization, the more his interest in politics grew. He saw a mounting need for the defense of personal liberties throughout the world, and for some reason, he was deeply troubled by it.

THOUGH THE DISTANCE between them stretched for hundreds of miles, Jim never forgot about the girl named Karen Sweet.

She was still in New Hampshire, completing her three-year program at the Bible school where they'd met. Determined to stay in touch, Jim wrote to her nearly every day, even making a few trips to New England to visit her during school breaks.

Evelyn Jacobson was thrilled with the relationship. She had suspected for some time that Jim had a romantic interest, although he was private about the details of it at first. When she learned that Karen was the object of his affection, she encouraged Jim to wait for her, in spite of the distance between them. In her opinion, Karen Sweet was the perfect girl for her son.

The Sweets were just as fond of Jim, and consented without hesitation when he finally sought permission to date their daughter. Although they both knew that marriage wouldn't be practical before Jim's college graduation, Jim proposed to Karen in June of 1985.

Karen completed Bible school and returned home to Fairfax, Virginia, where she took a job at a day care center to save money for the upcoming wedding. By the time Jim graduated from the University of Michigan in the spring of 1986, the Jacobson-Sweet wedding was just a few weeks away. After years of enduring a long distance relationship, Jim and Karen were married on May 17, 1986.

It was a traditional ceremony, held in front of 350 guests in a small New England church. They honeymooned briefly in Niagara Falls before settling into their first home in North Branch, Michigan, full of anticipation of the new life that was to come.

Armed with a mutual commitment to serve God unconditionally, Jim and Karen Jacobson had no idea of just how deeply they would draw on the strength of that vow just a few weeks into their new marriage.

Light in a Dark Place

People like Ronald Reagan came along back in '76. I went to the Republican Convention in Detroit when I was very young, just to attend. I wasn't a delegate, but I was there, and I did whatever I could for Reagan back when he took on Gerald Ford.

Here was a guy talking about, "You're not the problem, government's the problem." And boy, that made a lot of sense. This guy was the right man at the time, and a lot of young people got involved with Reagan and what he had to say about the role of the individual, and that rights come from God, and nobody else was talking about that. And then he paved the way for a lot of people who ran for office at the state and local levels, who started to say things about less government and less taxes. Before Reagan, nobody talked about lowering taxes or that we had too many regulations. And he started a revolution, if you will, what they called the Reagan Revolution. So many young people just grabbed hold of that, because it made so much sense...it was an exciting time.

Ronald Reagan just lifted everybody's spirits, the spirit of the nation. It was very captivating, especially for young conservatives at that time. He lost to Gerald Ford in '76, but

*he came back again. Today somebody like Reagan wouldn't
stand a chance, but at that time, it was exactly right.*

Jim Jacobson

AS JIM JACOBSON'S life was just beginning in the
United States, Chinese Christians on the other side of
the world were in the throes of a spiritual battle that
would affect their own nation for generations to come.

It started in 1949, when Mao Tse-Tung's Communist regime came into power, and religion took on a
new meaning in China. As foreign missionaries were
being expelled from the country, both Protestants and
Anglicans were forced to dissolve their denominations
and unite under the Three-Self Patriotic Movement
(TSPM) — a "religious" organization operating under
the concept of "self-administration, self-support, and
self-propagation." The Church was strictly ordered to
disassociate itself from any and all "imperialist" contact, and to submit to the authority of the Communist
Party. Churches now came under the control of the
TSPM, which would become a key instrument in the
government's attempt to maintain a tight grip on religion throughout the country. Under the TSPM, it was
forbidden to teach about Creation, judgment, the Second Coming, gifts of the Spirit, or even the resurrection.

Many Christians were concerned about submission
to a state-controlled church, and with good reason. The
idea of an atheist government having control over their
religious body did not sit well with the majority of Chinese believers. But as it was turning out, they were left
with no choice: anyone who refused to submit to the
TSPM was subject to arrest and imprisonment.   As

Communism spread across the land like a dark shadow, more and more believers abandoned the government's church and began conducting secret meetings in their homes.

By 1966, things had gotten progressively worse. The Cultural Revolution had begun, and Mao Tse-Tung's Red Guards were on a mission to destroy anything — or anyone — that opposed the ruthless leader or his communist teachings. All religious activities were banned, and nearly every church in the country was either closed or destroyed. Even the TSPM had disappeared. According to Mao Tse-Tung's wife, Christianity had "gone to the history museum" in China.

For those who held firmly to their belief in Jesus Christ, the persecution increased sevenfold. Many went to jail; those who could escaped overseas. Thousands of clergy, including TSPM pastors, were shipped off to labor camps. Hundreds of believers were simply executed. It was a desperate situation, and yet, despite the grave risk of imprisonment or martyrdom, the underground house church grew by leaps and bounds. Christianity, it seemed, was going to survive in communist China after all.

By the late 1970's, the Cultural Revolution was over. In an effort to demonstrate to the Western world that its country was attempting to establish a policy of religious freedom, the Chinese government ordered the release of many of its Christian prisoners. For a few brief years, even the expanding house churches enjoyed a time of relative peace.

By 1980, however, the TSPM was back, this time under the leadership of a liberal theologian and former Anglican named Nanjing Bishop Ding Guangxun. Under Bishop Ding, government-approved seminaries underwent a theological "reconstruction" campaign, which changed the focus of Christian teachings from justification by faith in Christ to justification by good deeds.

Under the new TSPM, it was of the utmost importance that all religious messages be made compatible with socialism. Once again, that meant that pastors were forbidden to preach about the divinity of Jesus Christ, His miracles or His resurrection. The TSPM also dictated what buildings were suitable for church services, which pastors were fit to preach, and what areas they were allowed to travel into. Church activities were restricted to Sunday services; mid-week meetings or Bible studies were not allowed, and certainly no gatherings in private homes. As a matter of fact, religious activities of any sort were forbidden outside of church buildings. Congregation members were also forbidden to have any contact with overseas church groups, to read any foreign Christian literature, listen to foreign Christian tapes, or tune in to gospel radio programs. Teachers, students, and anyone holding a military or government position was not allowed to embrace the faith.

Most of all, the State was the head of the Church, not Jesus Christ.

It was a religious crackdown that drove Christians into the underground church by the thousands. But for those who refused to officially "register" with the TSPM, being a Christian was now more dangerous than ever. If caught doing anything illegal they would face persecution, manifested in the form of monetary fines, arrest or imprisonment.

But the torture and abuse was the worst, especially in the prisons and labor camps. Hundreds of Christians who'd been apprehended for their faith were often forced to endure beatings with a variety of objects, including fists, batons—especially electric ones—poles, and even chairs or bats. Some were hung from the ceiling by their wrists, then tied in excruciatingly painful positions for hours on end. Sleep deprivation was also common, where in many cases Christians were forced to stand throughout the night without closing their eyes. Other believers were put in close fitting cages, then clawed to death by wild dogs or left outdoors for hours in the freezing cold.

Conditions in the labor camps were especially appalling. Prisoners were forced to endure long work hours, usually 5:00 a.m. to 11:00 p.m., struggling under grueling conditions to meet exceedingly high quotas or risk more painful beatings. Toilet facilities were completely inadequate, and prisoners were allowed to use them only a couple of specified times each day. Food was minimal at best, and barely enough to survive on.

And yet, despite the harshness of their lives, millions of believers continued to gather secretly—in caves, abandoned buildings, or wherever they were able—as their unwavering faith generated a small light in the dark place called China. They met to pray, read whatever copies of the Scriptures they had, and to draw strength in fellowship with one another, ever hopeful that, somehow, freedom would one day reign in their homeland.

NORTH BRANCH, MICHIGAN was the first place Jim and Karen Jacobson would call home following their wedding in May of 1986.

But Michigan was not where the newlyweds intended to put down roots. Jim had always dreamed of living in Florida, a desire that stemmed partly from his love of warm weather. With a cousin's help, he landed a teaching position at a school near Zephyrhills, Florida, and for a short while, Jim and Karen's plans seemed final: they would head south to begin their new life together.

But it was just a few weeks later when a sudden turn of events changed the course of their lives forever.

It was a day in early June, one that started just like any other day. Jim and Karen, with the help of Jim's brother-in-law, Brian, had spent part of the afternoon inspecting a trailer they intended to purchase in preparation for the move to Florida. It was also Brian's 30th birthday, and the family planned to throw a party in his honor.

No one could have known that, when Brian left his own party to run a brief errand that evening, he would never return. Killed by a drunk driver just a few miles from home, he left behind a wife—Jim's sister, Karen—and two small children.

The news was absolutely devastating for the Jacobsons. Brian had been a beloved member of the family for years, and it was almost impossible to believe that he was gone. For Jim, who had always regarded Brian as the brother he'd never had, the loss was especially painful. And he grieved deeply for his sister, who now had to face the overwhelming task of raising a five-year-old son and a five-month-old baby daughter by herself.

As the family banded together for strength and support, Jim and Karen realized that, in the blink of an eye, life had changed for them as well. Jim would not leave his sister or her children behind in her time of need, and the sunny skies of Florida seemed to be a distant reality now. The decision was obvious: he and Karen would remain in Michigan, at least for the time being.

Jim took a teaching position at North Branch Christian Academy—ironically, the same school he'd been expelled from as a wayward teenager. He taught high school math and history, for a starting salary of just $8,900 per year. It was his first teaching position, and Jim found that he truly enjoyed the ability to shape the minds and opinions of others, especially on the occasions when he received positive feedback from the students, or prayed with one of them about some personal difficulty in their life. But his meager salary as a private schoolteacher was simply not enough to live on, and Jim eventually took a second job at a vocational school, teaching word processing in an adult computer class. It was well outside the realm of his experience, but for $13 an hour, he was desperate for the additional income.

Over the ensuing months, Jim spent a great deal of time with his sister and her children. His own heart had been broken by the loss of her husband, and Jim knew that things would never quite be the same again. Brian had been an attendant in his wedding just weeks before his death, and now Jim could hardly look at photos from the event without being overwhelmed by his own sorrow.

The intensity of Jim's grief would keep him in his own dark place for years to come, but all was not lost from the tragedy. Out of the shadows of despair, God was refining in His servant an intense compassion for the widow and the fatherless that would later be used in a most unexpected way.

IT WAS THE summer of 1987 when Jim's father-in-law, Bob Sweet, then a White House staffer for President Ronald Reagan, approached Jim with an interesting question. A position was available in the U.S. Department of Education, and would he ever consider taking a job in Washington D.C.?

At first, the answer seemed obvious. Jim's teaching career was barely a year old, but his fascination with politics was still as great as ever. He'd spent an endless amount of time working on various projects and campaigns as a Young Republican, and he was an avid supporter of Ronald Reagan and his policies. But there was still his teaching to consider, something to which he and Karen had already committed their lives. And the prospect of relocating to Florida was still a possibility someday. But after more thought, Jim and Karen decided that the opportunity was too great to pass up. Jim would interview for the position in Washington, and if all went well, they would see how things turned out in one year's time.

Bob arranged an interview with Carol Whitten, the Director of Bilingual Education and Minority Languages Affairs, for the position of a Confidential Assistant in the Department of Education. It was both an exciting and overwhelming experience for Jim, and fortunately, he and Carol immediately hit it off. The interview went well—so well, in fact, that she offered him the job.

The next step was to pass through a lengthy background check, a process conducted by the Political Affairs Office in the White House and something that was required for all political appointees. Among other things, Jim had to prove that he supported Ronald Reagan, which he could easily do, and especially that he wasn't a member of the Communist party. As the process was being finalized, Jim and Karen located a small rental home in Fairfax, Virginia, a metropolitan area 17 miles outside of Washington.

It was the break of a lifetime for a young college graduate, and Jim was grateful to his father-in-law for initiating such an opportunity. Washington was intensely fast-paced and unlike anything he'd ever experienced, but Jim quickly realized that it was the kind of environment he thrived on.

Less than a year later, another opportunity presented itself in his rising political career. Gary Bauer, who served as Ronald Reagan's Undersecretary of Education and was Jim's supervisor in the Department, changed positions to become an advisor on domestic policy. The rearrangement created new opportunities for others in political positions, including Jim. Under Gary Bauer's direction, he was promoted to the position of policy analyst in the White House Office of Policy Development.

It was almost too incredible to believe. After years of nurturing a lifelong dream, it had finally become a reality. Jim was a White House staff member, working for the most powerful leader in the world: the American president. It was especially exciting to work for Ronald Reagan, a leader he'd always admired. Reagan was in his second term, having been re-elected by a landslide in 1984. He was outspoken in his anti-Communist views, and his negotiations with Soviet leader Mikhail Gorbachev had been instrumental in bringing about a peaceful end to the longstanding Cold War. Reagan was also a devout Christian, and tended to stress policies that promoted the family unit. He was outspokenly pro-life, and was an avid supporter of voluntary prayer in public schools, issues that were close to Jim's own heart. On the occasions when he participated in meetings with the President, Jim always found the man to be truly genuine, someone with whom he could easily hold a conversation.

Jim worked well with everyone in the administration, where he was learning the ins and outs of government procedures, as well as policies on foreign and domestic affairs. It was invaluable experience, and for Jim, working in the White House was also a tremendous privilege. It was an exciting time in American history, and he was honored to be a part of it.

AS JIM'S POLITICAL career was growing, so was the Jacobson family.

On September 6, 1988, Karen gave birth to their first child, a girl whom they named Kierstin Aura. Jim stayed in the delivery room for the entire birth, although he would have been more than happy to forego witnessing the event altogether. He had a phobia of needles, and he especially didn't like to see Karen in pain, but for her sake managed to overcome his reservations to be by her side during the momentous event.

From the outset of their marriage, it had been understood that Karen would stay home to raise any children that God saw fit to give them. Motherhood was both a pleasure and her calling in life, and Karen had no qualms about fulfilling her role as a wife and mother. Although Jim's work schedule was long and demanding, often keeping him absent from the evening dinner table, the family still managed to enjoy quality time together, especially on the weekends. Karen, who was simply grateful that her husband had a good, well-paying job that provided for their needs, often employed her parents' help on the many occasions when Jim was not at home.

But by 1988, Vice President George Bush was elected as Reagan's presidential successor, and Jim's position with the Reagan administration was coming to an end. What had been a one-year "trial" period in Washington for Jim and Karen stretched into a second year as, by February of 1989, Jim had secured a new position on Capitol Hill.

U.S. Senator Gordon J. Humphrey was in his second term in office when Jim was hired to become his legislative assistant. Humphrey, who had served in the Air Force and worked as a professional pilot before pursuing a political career, sat on the Committee for Foreign Relations, the Armed Services Committee, and was a leader in the Congressional Task Force on Afghanistan. He had also become a Christian during his tenure in the Senate, and he and Jim were destined to become good friends.

Much of Jim's work as a legislative assistant centered on the pro-life movement, an issue that the Senator strongly supported. The Hyde Amendment had been restricting the government funding of abortions since 1976, and Jim enjoyed assisting Humphrey with writing portions of law that continued to ensure the clampdown on the American abortion industry.

Jim's job on Capitol Hill was as busy as the days were long. He would often leave for work around 7:30 a.m. and not return home until late that evening, or sometimes even early the next morning. He and Karen attended a large nondenominational church in Fairfax, but the demands of the job didn't leave much time for any other activities — church related or otherwise. They'd had their second child in 1990, another daughter named Kelly May, and the demands at home were growing. But life was serious on the Hill, and Jim was in the big league now. If he was going to last in Washington, he either had to keep up or get left behind. He was grateful for Karen's loving and unconditional support of his career, and knew without a doubt that none of it would be possible without her.

Although he enjoyed his work for Senator Humphrey, Jim had known from the outset that his position as a legislative assistant would be short-lived. Humphrey had already announced that he would not run for a third senatorial term, and by 1991 Jim was faced with the task of finding another job. After a brief lapse in employment, he obtained a position in the Bush administration, working as a political appointee in the Management and Budget Office in the Department of Education.

But a new presidential election was coming up, and things weren't looking too good for George Bush Sr. His popularity among the American people had fallen dramatically in the wake of an economic recession and the perceived failure of Operation Desert Storm, and his approval rating had dropped to just over 40 percent by election time. Jim, along with others in the administration, began watching the polls carefully, ever mindful of what would happen in the event of a loss.

Against all hope, the inevitable occurred. Arksansas Governor Bill Clinton went on to claim 43% of the vote in the 1992 run for president, defeating George Bush and Independent party member Ross Perot. His victory ended a 12-year Republican reign in the White House, giving Democrats full control of Congress, the Senate, and the House of Representatives.

Jim watched the results come in on election night with a sinking feeling. The possibility had been looming for months, and now it was a stark reality: he was out of a job. The past few years had come and gone in a whirlwind, and there had been many opportunities he'd never imagined having in his lifetime. Now, just like that, his career in Washington seemed to have disappeared in a cloud of smoke.

Jim had promised God long ago that he would follow His lead wherever it took him, and it was a commitment he still intended to keep. But with a wife and two young children depending on him, Jim knew that another window of opportunity had to open...and fast.

Christian Solidarity

If I hadn't had the experience as a young man in my mid and early twenties, working with some of the most powerful people in the world and exposed to the things that I was exposed to, to understand how government works, how other governments work and don't work and how things get done, I never would have been prepared for what I'm doing now. I never would have had the contacts that I have, not only here domestically, but around the world.

It shaped the direction of this organization, where we combine advocacy work in Washington with humanitarian aid. If I hadn't had that personal involvement in understanding how Capitol Hill and the Executive Branch work, we just wouldn't be involved in it. It's an intimidating, mysterious process for most people outside of Washington. But once you're in it, and know how it works, you feel confident with trying to bring pressure where pressure can be brought. It's made all the difference in the world.

Jim Jacobson

Zurich, Switzerland
1975

HIS NAME WAS George Vins, and it was a name that the Reverend Hans-Jung Stuckelberger wouldn't soon forget.

Stuckelberger had gotten word that Vins, a Baptist pastor and leader in the Soviet Union's underground church, was facing a third prison sentence for the crime of preaching the Gospel in the Communist nation. Although he'd never met the man, the resilience of his comrade's faith in the face of such harsh suffering made a deep impression on Stuckelberger. As a show of solidarity for Vins and all persecuted Christians around the world, he assembled a series of peaceful demonstrations and prayer services in Zurich and Berne.

Encouraged by the overwhelming support for the cause, Stuckelberger and his associates founded a ministry committed to providing both aid and advocacy for persecuted Christians on April 15, 1977. The organization, comprised of hundreds of Christians from various denominations, was aptly named Christian Solidarity International. As the organization grew, it established affiliate offices in the Czech Republic, France, Germany, Hungary, Italy, South Korea, the Netherlands, and by 1983, the USA. Its primary objective, according to Article 18 of the U.N.'s Universal Declaration of Human Rights, was based on the belief that "everyone has the right to freedom...to change his religion or belief, and freedom, either alone or in community with others and in public or private, to manifest his religion or belief in teaching, practice, worship and observance."

AS JIM'S WORK in Washington was coming to an end in 1992, a national crisis was paving the way for a new opportunity to work alongside his father-in-law, Bob Sweet.

As Director of the National Institute for Education during the Reagan administration from 1982 to 1983, Bob had become aware of the growing problem of illiteracy in the United States. Much of his information came through the work of the Reading Reform Foundation, a nonprofit, educational organization that had been established in 1961 for the purpose of combating illiteracy. The organization's research, which revealed that the "whole language" method for reading instruction was largely responsible for declining literacy scores, became Bob's introduction to the magnitude of the problem.

Despite strong scientific evidence that supported the importance of phonics-based reading instruction, the "whole language" philosophy had been used in the American school system for decades; as a result, an astounding 23 million Americans were struggling with literacy, and the number was climbing. Throughout his remaining tenure in Washington, Bob pursued a national re-education about effective reading instruction, commissioning the report *Becoming a Nation of Readers*, publishing several of his own articles, and laying the foundation for the 1992 National Adult Literacy Survey, the largest literacy assessment ever funded by the federal government.

Bob had been sharing his concerns with Jim about the country's reading crisis for some time, until they finally came to a decision: they would launch their own organization to help promote phonics-based reading instruction. On January 8, 1993, the National Right to

Read Foundation (NRRF) was officially established. Through the ongoing provision of information and resources to teachers and the American public about the proven benefits of phonics-based instruction, NRRF's mission was to help ensure that most American children would be able to read by the end of first grade, and become proficient readers by the end of third grade at the latest.

Jim willingly entered into the venture with his father-in-law, having personally seen for himself the effects of children struggling with reading disabilities. But running a nonprofit was a completely new challenge for Jim, and as NRRF's vice-president and co-founder, he was responsible for launching the organization's initial fundraising efforts, assembling a mailing list, and putting together its newsletter, *The Right to Read Report*. It was hard work, but as hundreds—and eventually thousands—of parents began calling in to NRRF's helpline with stories of how their otherwise bright children had somehow missed out on learning how to read, there was a new realization of how desperately the organization's services were truly needed.

Although his work with the NRRF was both an interesting and invaluable experience, Jim was ready to move on two years later. By that time Karen had given birth to their third child, James, and the organization was just barely generating enough funds to support both the Sweets and their own growing family. The lack of sufficient income had already forced Jim and Karen to sell their Fairfax townhouse and move into a small, three-bedroom ranch home near Front Royal, for a rent of just $700 per month. There was no doubt about it: money was tight.

Jim took a series of odd jobs in an effort to make ends meet, including a consulting project for Bill Hansen, his former supervisor in the Department of Education. He also worked on an extensive research project for Michael Farris, a constitutional lawyer whom he'd met and befriended during his time on Capitol Hill. Mike was the founder and president of the Home School Legal Defense Association, a national organization dedicated to defending the civil rights of homeschooling parents.

In the fall of 1995, Jim got an unusual phone call from his friend. Mike was chairman of the board for an organization called Christian Solidarity International USA, a Swiss-based ministry that aided Christians around the world who were persecuted for their faith. CSI USA was in need of a new executive director, and would Jim be interested in the job?

It was an offer that Jim wasn't expecting, though it certainly sounded like an interesting prospect. Mike had established CSI's United States office with the help of Faith Whittlesey, a former U.S. ambassador to Switzerland and director of the Office of Public Liaison during the Reagan administration. He and Faith were looking for someone who would help them re-establish the efficiency of the organization with a more conservative, Biblical approach than its Swiss parent. Mike seemed confident that Jim was ideal for the job, and with good reason: a large part of the position would entail lobbying on Capitol Hill—a process that Jim knew very well—for the rights of persecuted Christians.

Jim thoughtfully considered the opportunity. He had just recently gotten another, more lucrative job offer from Bill Hansen, who had established a new lobbying firm on K Street in Washington. Taking a job with another nonprofit would mean less income, although at least the organization had been receiving full subsidized funding from its Swiss headquarters. Becoming the executive director of Christian Solidarity didn't seem to be as promising for his political career, but the more Jim thought about it, the more the idea of helping suffering Christians overseas became too intriguing to pass up. Somehow, working for CSI seemed to be the right thing to do.

With Karen's support and encouragement, Jim accepted Mike's offer. It was a decision that marked another turning point in his life, although its impact wouldn't truly begin to manifest for some time. But after eighteen months of going without stable, salaried employment, his job with CSI USA was, first and foremost, another means of income for himself and his family.

Or so it seemed at the time.

JOHN EIBNER, CHRISTIAN Solidarity International's Director of Human Rights, was on a mission.

Reports from Sudan, a country that for years had been overwhelmed by civil war, were indicating that the centuries-old practice of slave raiding was once again on the rise. Arab raiders from the north were swooping down on villages in the south, kidnapping thousands and forcing them into bondage.

Women and children who'd been abducted in the raids were roped by the neck or strapped to animals before being forced on the long march back north. Many girls were gang raped along the way; children who refused to be silent were shot on the spot. All were forced into a life of slavery after reaching their destination, where they were either kept by militia soldiers or sold in the markets. Boys were often put to work as livestock herders, forced to sleep with the animals they cared for. Women and girls were used as domestics by day and concubines by night. More often than not, their masters gave them new, Arabic names and forced them to pray as Muslims, stripping them of their own religious or cultural identity.

A tall, thin, dark-skinned people, the Dinkas were caught in the center of the conflict. Although they were the largest group in the south, making up over ten percent of Sudan's population, they were looked down on by many other Sudanese people, particularly their lighter-skinned counterparts. They were leaders in the country's devastating civil war, comprising a majority of the rebel army that was fighting the government's Islamic militia. They were also unpopular because of their large Christian population, although Christian was a name that seemed more appropriate on a cultural basis rather than a spiritual one.

But regardless of how Christianity applied to them, it was a factor that kept them living under harsh oppression and persecution at the hands of the Islamic government. The surge in slave raiding had become part of a government campaign to Islamize all of southern Sudan; now, scores of Dinkas were being carried away in the process, only to suffer unspeakable atrocities at the hands of their captors. But eventually, Dinkas who had somehow managed to live freely in the north began secretly working to locate their abducted children and negotiate their return, while those left behind in the south began their own quest to scrounge together whatever money they could to buy back the freedom of other long-lost relatives.

At first, the reports about slavery were hard to believe, especially in the face of the Sudanese government's insistent denials that the practice even existed. But as more eyewitnesses continued stepping forward, aid workers in the region began to think differently about the situation. One thing, however, was certain — if the stories were true, then the world needed to know about it.

John Eibner was determined to make that happen. In direct defiance of the Sudanese government, he chartered a plane and flew into the deepest region of the country in May of 1995, where he met with dozens of Dinka women who told him all about the plight of their abducted children. Their testimonies were all he needed to move into action. He returned to Switzerland, challenging journalists around the world to make the trek into Sudan and document the slave trade for themselves. Before long, the word was spreading like wildfire: slavery had reared its ugly head in Sudan. As the outrage ignited, mostly among Christians and African Americans, Christian Solidarity International began leading the efforts to aid those caught in the Sudanese slave trade. The plan, at first, seemed relatively simple, and in fact built on the practice that the Dinkas themselves were already using — to buy back the freedom of as many men, women and children as humanly possible.

As the new executive director of CSI USA, slave redemption would soon move to the top of Jim's to-do list. But despite the fact that such a grave atrocity was being committed in Sudan, a more imminent problem was staring him in the face: there was no money in the organization's coffer.

Shortly after taking on the position, Jim had traveled to Zurich, Switzerland for his first CSI conference, where he quickly learned about the Swiss headquarters' true intentions for the United States office. Instead of being merely a lobbyist for the organization, the Swiss had, in fact, wanted the U.S. branch to begin funding programs with its own money—a detail that had never been made clear to Jim, by anyone, before he'd signed up for the job. But the problem was that, having historically relied on the Swiss for one hundred percent of its financing, the United States had no real, immediate way to generate its own funds. Although Jim's predecessor, an evangelical minister named Steve Snyder, had never been concerned with the issues of fundraising or acquiring donors, the truth hit Jim like a ton of bricks: the overwhelming task of building up the organization, almost from scratch, had suddenly fallen on him.

At Jim's insistence, the Swiss finally agreed to accommodate the U.S. with a two-year start-up grant—monthly seed money that was to be used for salaries, fundraising, and other expenses until the office became self-sufficient. There was a lot of work to be done, but at least the grant would help—it was certainly better than nothing. Still, Jim couldn't help but wonder what he'd gotten himself into. Things were definitely not what they had seemed to be.

DENNIS BALCOMBE, AN American missionary who had moved to Hong Kong shortly after the Vietnam War, had a fascinating story to tell.

A guest speaker at the CSI conference in Zurich, Dennis introduced himself as the senior pastor of Revival Christian Church. RCC sponsored a program called Donkeys for Jesus, a ministry that smuggled desperately needed Bibles into China. Scores of Chinese Christians were being severely persecuted by their Communist government, and for most of them, copies of the Scriptures were incredibly hard to come by.

Over the years, Dennis had personally delivered thousands of Bibles into China's underground church. He'd been caught, arrested and subsequently blacklisted from the country for his work, but his ministry was still as active—and necessary—as ever. As Jim listened raptly to Dennis's accounts of the spirit-filled Christians that were crowding China's house churches, he knew without a doubt that it was something he wanted to learn more about for himself.

Jim was already aware of the problems that existed in China, a country that, despite its overwhelming track record for human rights violations, was continually granted trade relations by the United States government each year. The country's 1989 Tiananmen Square massacre and its forced abortion and sterilization policies were only part of the atrocities that its government carried out in the name of Communism; now, the compelling urgency of Dennis's stories about Christians who were being imprisoned, tortured, or shipped to "re-education" camps in China were too remarkable to ignore.

Over a dinner meeting, Dennis invited Jim to an upcoming Donkeys for Jesus conference in Hong Kong—a conference where he would not only learn about evangelism in China, but how to "secretly" deliver Bibles into areas of the country where they were most needed. Jim returned home to the United States, already anticipating the trip. Somehow, his meeting with Dennis Balcombe had sparked unforgettable intrigue about a body of nameless, faceless, suffering Christians on the other side of the world, whose testimonies of miraculous healings and unwavering faith made them seem as if they hailed right from the pages of the New Testament itself.

Something was going on in China, and Jim intended to find out.

Into the Underground

I fell in love with China and its people. The house church in China is so vibrant, and their faith is so exciting, explosive and dynamic...it's an opportunity that I hope everyone would have, to go into the underground house church in China. It just does something to your own faith.

But it was like a reality shock for me, because when you grow up as an American with the freedom that we have, you don't even think about it. It just made me realize for the first time, in a very dramatic way, what a difference it was. Just the thought that I could be arrested for having a Bible or for attending church, or that I would have to take a risk for my family, or that I may never see my kids again...it blew me away. And I was just galvanized to do this kind of work. They're worth it...they're worth helping.

Jim Jacobson

Guangzhou, China
July, 1995

IT WAS A dangerous mission, and the four men knew it. But the contraband inside the large, heavy bags they carried was of vital importance to hundreds of men and women on the other side, and it was a risk they were willing to take.

The train to Henan was especially crowded that day, so the men were forced to stand during the long, four-hour ride. But in a matter of moments, the uneventful trip took a dramatic turn when, after a policeman entered the train during a brief stop, he approached the men and asked why they were carrying so many bags.

They were porters, they answered, hired by someone to deliver the bags into Henan. When the officer skeptically asked them to open the luggage, the men told him there were no keys for the locks; nevertheless, the policeman insisted.

The officer peered in silence at the contents of the first bag, then opened the others before realizing that they all held the same thing—copies of a book titled *The Shepherd's Staff*. What, he demanded suspiciously, were these books for?

To teach people how to shepherd, the men replied, but the officer wasn't convinced. Upon further inspection, he quickly realized that the book—three hundred copies of it—was in fact a Christian devotional.

Furious at the deception, the officer ordered the men to follow him into the train's restaurant. In a split second, the men knew that the situation had taken a turn for the worse: they were about to be arrested.

As the policeman moved ahead of them through the crowded train, the men knew that they only had a matter of moments to act. Abandoning the bags on the floor of the car, two of the men jumped out a nearby window while the other two ran in the opposite direction. They continued to race through the congested rail cars, then finally jumped out another window once the train slowed to a halt at a small, nearby station.

Free from the train's confines, the two men continued running until they reached a mountain. As they climbed to the top, they instinctively knelt down and lifted up a prayer of thanksgiving. Although they were deeply saddened about not being able to deliver the devotionals to their Christian brothers and sisters in Henan, they were overwhelmingly grateful for God's protection—because, that quickly, all four of them had been spared from an unthinkable fate.

It was just one more day in the underground church in China.

THE CITY OF Hong Kong, once a small, out-of-the-way fishing village off the southern coast of China, was destined to become one of the world's greatest tourist attractions.

Having thrived under British rule since the 19th century, the city was a hub for international business, becoming the world's busiest deep-water harbor and even the banking capital of Asia. Its profusion of high rise buildings and congested streets were evidence of the city's grossly overcrowded living conditions, making it one of the most densely populated regions in the world. Although its ethnic and religious diversity contributed to the fact that it had grown into one of Asia's most cosmopolitan cities, its predominantly Chinese population remained strongly rooted in Buddhist beliefs and traditions.

As he arrived in Hong Kong's bustling airport in early 1996, Jim was immediately overwhelmed by a sense of culture shock. He'd made the 30-hour trip from America to attend the Donkeys for Jesus conference, an event that he and Karen had been anticipating with hesitation as well as excitement. Neither of them was sure of what to expect, especially since the trip was not sponsored by Christian Solidarity International. And yet, months after having met Dennis Balcombe in Switzerland and learning about China's persecuted church, it was a trip that, without a doubt, Jim still felt compelled to take. So, with as much money as the Jacobsons could raise or scrape together, Jim purchased an airline ticket to Asia.

He'd come to Hong Kong with a few pieces of luggage, a small amount of money, and not much else. He had Dennis Balcombe's address, although Jim had no idea of where to start looking for him. Asking for directions seemed to be a nearly impossible feat—hardly anyone, it seemed, spoke English, and he certainly didn't speak Chinese. With such an obvious language barrier, Jim doubted that he could even make a telephone call.

Using the public transportation system was an equally intimidating prospect, so Jim decided to simply begin walking. Luggage in tow, he maneuvered his way through the busy, jam-packed streets, wondering how in the world he would ever find Dennis.

Unfamiliar sights and sounds were all around him. Temples and shrines honoring a variety of Buddhist deities lined the streets, the pungent smell of burning incense wafting from their small, dark hallways. Outdoor vendors were cooking on little carts, mixing food with a strange variety of rice, garlic and other spices. The few public restrooms Jim managed to find were unlike anything he'd ever seen before. But most of all, he was simply amazed at the sheer volume of *people* that were hurrying all around him. It was hard to believe that so much humanity could live and exist in such a small amount of space.

DENNIS BALCOMBE, BORN and raised in California, had discovered Jesus Christ at the age of sixteen.

He attended the Assemblies of God Southern California Bible College after high school graduation, then was later drafted into the Army and sent overseas to Vietnam. While on leave from his military duties in 1967, he felt compelled to pay a visit to Hong Kong, where the chaotic disorder from China's Cultural Revolution had spilled into nearby streets. The situation seemed hopeless, and yet Dennis prayed that God would one day return him to Hong Kong to build a ministry that would bless the people of China.

The prayer came to fruition by 1969, when Dennis was finally discharged from the Army. He returned to Hong Kong, immersing himself in the culture by moving into an area where no other foreigners could be found. Within eight months, he had learned enough Cantonese to start a church.

Despite the fierce opposition to Christianity that surrounded it on all sides, Revival Christian Church thrived quickly. While it was certainly remarkable that his church in Hong Kong was growing at such a rapid pace, Dennis and his colleagues had been praying patiently for God to once again open the doors to China. When the country finally established its "Open Door

Policy" in 1978, Dennis was on one of the first tours into the mainland.

It would be the first of over 500 trips. By 1988, Dennis was deeply involved in the mentoring of China's house church pastors, often ministering to hundreds of them at a time for 12 hours a day, several days in a row. A Pentecostal movement was sweeping through the underground church, and in the course of his ministry Dennis had the privilege of witnessing the sort of miracles that only fervent, spirit-filled faith — the kind that belonged to thousands of China's persecuted Christians — could produce.

As Revival Christian Church's membership grew into the hundreds, its ministries would expand into countries such as India, Vietnam, Malaysia, Cambodia and Nepal, among many others. And yet, Dennis Balcombe and his team of ministers, teachers, evangelists and missionaries remained committed to Hong Kong and the Chinese people more than ever before. In time, one of the church's main ministries would focus on the provision of Bibles and other teaching materials to the scores of unregistered house churches scattered throughout China. The ministry was called Donkeys for Jesus, and it would be instrumental in successfully smuggling millions of urgently needed Bibles into the country. And, just as faithfully, hundreds of people from around the world would travel into Hong Kong each year to participate in the ministry.

But the work was not without its danger. Many of Dennis's Chinese co-workers received lengthy prison sentences for their part in illegal Bible distribution; some were even martyred. Just weeks after a 1994 adoption of new government regulations that tightened restrictions on places of worship in China, Dennis himself was arrested and expelled from the country because of his association with an exposed house church. He would subsequently tell the story of his capture before a U.S. Congressional committee and the Secretary of State, and even receive extensive media coverage throughout Hong Kong. But in the end, the word was final: Dennis was forever forbidden from entering China, the country that he loved so deeply.

THE DONKEYS FOR Jesus conference was held in Revival Christian Church, a large, townhouse-type structure situated in the urban region of Kowloon. It had taken nearly half a day — and miles of walking — for Jim to finally locate it, and he'd come away from the experience with a new appreciation of just how big Hong Kong truly was.

He had also managed to rent a room in an inexpensive guest house, and despite the difficulties of his first few hours in Hong Kong, it was exciting to be a part of the conference. He was among 50 other attendees, many of whom had traveled from Australia, the Philippines, and Canada, to learn how to become a "donkey for Jesus" and participate in such an important ministry.

The conference's two-day agenda was filled with prayer services, informational sessions about traveling into China, and preparation for meeting with underground house churches. By the end of the conference, Jim had purchased 50 Chinese Bibles from Dennis.

With dire warnings about the danger of exposing contraband Bibles to the authorities fresh in his mind, Jim ventured onto the mainland with Dennis' son-in-law, who in turn would introduce him to house church pastors. He spent the next few days on a guarded mission, often meeting pastors on public buses. After they had carefully revealed their identities to each other, they would change buses and travel to a secret location where Jim could make the Bible delivery, looking furtively over their shoulders all the while to ensure that they weren't being followed. The entire scenario reminded Jim of an old spy movie, and he soon began to realize the utter seriousness of his actions. His inexperience in such an alien environment was surely causing him to stick out like a sore thumb, and yet, amazingly, the brave pastors seemed willing to risk everything, even their lives, to receive such a precious commodity.

To Jim, who'd come from a country where copies of the Scriptures were so plentiful that their very existence was taken for granted, it was a humbling realization.

BUGGING DEVICES WERE one more reminder of just how serious life truly was in China.

They're probably everywhere in here, the underground leaders informed Jim as they cranked up the radio volume in the shabby hotel room where they'd met. As they sat down to talk, Jim couldn't help but think about how annoying the strange, blaring Chinese music really was, though he knew it was necessary to keep their conversation private.

In fervent whispers that Jim had to strain to hear, the pastors told him all about life in the underground. For the thousands of Chinese Christians who chose not to belong to the government-sanctioned church, the threat of imprisonment was always an imminent risk. Besides owning an illegally obtained Bible, they could be arrested for anything from possessing illegal literature to having unlawful gatherings; sometimes, even the mere suspicion that they were participating in something illegal was enough to warrant arrest. As Jim listened incredulously, Pastor Wong told him all about his own arrest and imprisonment. He was the head of a rather large network of house churches, and the authorities had been determined to learn about the other underground leaders who were assisting him. They resorted to torture when he refused to disclose any information, systematically breaking each one of his fingers with a pair of pliers until he passed out.

Pastor Wong cried as he recounted the horrific events, until Jim was moved to tears himself. The pastor's disfigured hands testified of his story, so Jim knew that the heartbroken man was, indeed, telling the truth. As he continued listening to their accounts of torture, abuse, and the threat of re-education camps, Jim was being assured of one thing: he *belonged* in China. He belonged where persecution was refining the faith of hundreds of thousands of believers — men and women who were, in fact, *his* Christian brethren. And they were suffering beyond anything he'd ever remotely imagined.

Suddenly, everything that Jim had ever read or heard about persecution had become as real as the men sitting in front of him. Even the recent difficulties he'd experienced as the new director of Christian Solidarity International USA now paled in comparison to the reality that overwhelmed him. Millions of people around the world — in fact, millions of people in China alone — were enduring unspeakable hardships simply because of their faith in Jesus Christ, and for some reason God had uniquely prepared Jim to help them. From his political work in Washington D.C. to the daily grind of running a small nonprofit organization in Virginia, Jim now knew that his own life had been cultivated for the purpose of entering into this new calling: to help the persecuted.

And as long as Christians were being persecuted somewhere in the world, he would be right there on the frontlines of the battle with them.

A Forgotten People

I went to church with the Karen people. I heard them singing familiar hymns — the same hymns that we sang in our church back in Virginia — praying the same way, taking up an offering in a Baptist church. They're people who don't have anything, and I just had an instant bond with them. And then I started learning about their cause, that they're basically fighting for God and country, and I just kept getting more and more attached to their whole situation.

Jim Jacobson

JIM RETURNED TO the United States with a new sense of purpose. He knew he would never forget the things he saw and heard in China, and nothing was more important than getting the word out about the millions of suffering Christians overseas.

But if Christian Solidarity International USA was to ever get off the ground, fundraising was still the first order of business. The plan was to run the operation with the efficiency of a political campaign, and speaking engagements became a critical way for Jim to reach potential donors. After an exhausting workweek in his cramped, Washington-based office, he often spent his weekends traveling to churches as far away as Pennsylvania or even Florida, anywhere he'd been invited to speak about the persecuted church. He spent hours talking to congregations filled with people who had no idea about the severity—or even the existence—of Christian persecution, and what they could do about it as brothers and sisters in Christ. It was a revelation that pulled on the heartstrings of his listeners, many of whom thanked Jim afterwards for bringing such gravely important news through the doors of their sanctuary.

As the mailing list slowly grew, Jim and his assistant, a college student named Darren Jones, began the task of raising funds for the organization. As they cranked out direct mail pieces by the hundreds, it wouldn't be long before the Jacobsons found themselves setting up tables in the basement of their home to accommodate the never-ending piles of mailing supplies and fundraising letters.

Jim attended a second CSI conference in Switzerland, certain that the details of his recent fact-finding mission would generate the organization's interest in supporting the underground church in China. The reaction was disappointing, to say the least. In the wake of its first redemption expedition a few months earlier, Christian Solidarity International had become one of the leading humanitarian organizations entrenched in the battle to redeem slaves in Sudan, and support from individuals and churches alike were pouring in for one purpose: to buy back the freedom of as many enslaved souls as possible. Jim's main goal, as the new director of CSI USA, was to raise funds for slave redemption.

The priority was clear—and the priority, as far as CSI was concerned, was *not* the underground church in China.

MARTIN PANTER, A British-born doctor and president of CSI Australia, was Jim's roommate during the conference.

He told Jim the story about an ethnic tribe in Myanmar, a country also known as Burma. The Karen, historically known for their Christian roots, had been severely persecuted by their own government for decades. In an effort to escape the relentless violence and destruction, many of them were seeking refuge along the Burma-Thailand border. It was one of the most brutal ethnic cleansing attempts in history, and yet the world was hardly aware of it.

Dr. Panter told Jim about the legend of the Golden Book and the story of Adoniram Judson, the first American missionary to reach the Karen in the 1800's. He told him the account of the Karen's faithful allegiance to the British during World War II, and how they had been fighting for their own liberation ever since. The result of the longstanding civil war in Burma had left the country in ruins, with thousands of people now pining away in refugee camps.

Deeply involved in their cause, Dr. Panter had been visiting the Karen on medical and fact-finding missions since 1989. In 1995, soon after the Karen rebel army lost their last significant outpost in Kawmoora to the Burmese army, he had paid a visit to the family of Kawmoora's commander, Colonel Taou Lo, while the Colonel was on the front lines of battle. Colonel Lo, a Christian who often prayed with his troops via two-way radio, had once dreamed of an elderly man with his hands raised in front of him; on his left hand was the number 16, on his right hand was the number 85, and the number 101 was above his head. After praying about the dream's interpretation, the Colonel decided that he needed to read the Psalms — the only book in the Bible with either 101 verses or chapters. After reading through Psalms 16, 85 and 101, he plastered the walls of his bunker with their words, and even renamed his troops "Battalion 101," after Psalm 101's first verse: *I will sing of your love and justice to you, O Lord.* After Dr. Panter prayed with the Colonel's wife and 20-year-old daughter during his visit, he left their home knowing that, in some small way, he had been able to represent Jesus' love to them in such a dire time, and that he had, in fact, assured them of his commitment to stand in solidarity with the Karen.

Dr. Panter also ran a small orphanage for Karen children in a Thailand refugee camp, and more than once he invited Jim to come overseas to witness the situation for himself. As compelling as the story was, his doggedness about the matter was almost exasperating to Jim. The doctor felt that Jim, as an American, would be particularly interested in supporting the cause of the Karen, and in helping to expose the carnage that had gone seemingly unnoticed by most of the civilized world. After more of Dr. Panter's unrelenting persistence, Jim finally agreed to meet him overseas.

He was not even remotely prepared for what he would find in Thailand.

THE MAE LA refugee camp, located north of Mae Sot on the western border of Thailand, was home to tens of thousands of displaced Karen and Karenni men, women and children, including the children in Dr. Panter's orphanage.

Separated from Burma only by a mountain and a river, it was often said that the sound of landmines could be heard going off in the distance near Mae La, and the scent of battle seemed to hang in the air. It was the largest refugee camp in proximity to Mae Sot, and had become a place where thousands of people would endure a kind of poverty that those in the developed world could never begin to imagine.

The first desperate migrants began arriving at the border in 1984, after the Karen National Union lost its Wan Kha military base in the wake of a large-scale offensive strike by the Burmese army. As the Burmese continued to take control of new regions over the next 10 years, more Karen and Karenni people took flight into Thailand until, by 1994, over 80,000 refugees crowded the border. The growing population soon became a considerable problem for the Thai government, which, while sympathetic to their plight, was hesitant to allow them further access into the country.

And yet, as throngs of homeless people continued to swarm the area, new communities began to evolve, complete with schools, shops, churches, and even a water and sewage system. Hundreds of ramshackle huts stretched for miles along the road, evidence of the mass-scale displacement that was forcing so many to live their lives in limbo.

All of the refugee camps, including Mae La, were overcrowding quickly, thanks to the constant influx of new arrivals from Burma. It was an immense strain on the charities and non-governmental organizations that serviced the camps with medical care and other humanitarian aid, and despite the meager food rations supplied by the Burmese Border Consortium, many of the residents—especially the children—suffered from severe iron deficiencies and malnutrition, among other things.

It was the kind of dreary environment that, as they lost hope of ever returning to their homeland, kept some of Mae La's residents drowning their depression in homemade alcohol. They had already experienced more fear and heartache than it was ever thought possible, and now there was the unending hardship of life in a refugee camp to deal with. Even for the few who were granted work permits in Thailand, it was no secret that life as a migrant, earning as little as 20 percent of the Thai minimum wage, was not much better than life as a refugee.

Jim couldn't believe his eyes as he stared at the deplorable sight in front of him. Before Dr. Panter had told him about the Karen, he had never heard anything at all about such a horrific problem in a country called Burma. Now he was looking at an immense bamboo prison, where unbelievably, some of its inhabitants had resided for over 20 years. Some refugees had fled to the relative safety of the camp after their villages had been destroyed; others had escaped from captivity by the Burmese military after being forced to carry their equipment and supplies. But what seemed to be the most tragic reality of all was that many had been born in the camp, and many would likely die there. The more he learned, and the more people he talked to, Jim was becoming outraged by the entire situation.

Dr. Panter introduced Jim to Dr. Singh, a colleague who had also dedicated his life to helping the Karen. Dr. Singh, a Sikh Indian who was married to a Karen woman, had practiced medicine in Burma until the authorities informed him that he could no longer treat Karen people. When Dr. Singh defiantly replied that he would treat anyone who came into his emergency room, he was warned that he would be arrested and sent to prison if he disobeyed government orders. Dr. Singh and his family, along with other pro-democracy supporters, were subsequently forced to flee to the relative safety of the jungle to escape imprisonment.

The Singhs were eventually granted access into Thailand, where there was an overwhelming need for doctors to help treat the war-weary Karen. But circumstances were still dismal, and in a supreme act of parental love, the Singhs managed to find Christian families in Thailand to adopt their own four children. As difficult as the decision was, Dr. Singh and his wife knew that it was the only way that their children would not only remain safe, but would have opportunities to get an education.

Jim hit it off instantly with Dr. Singh. It was the beginning of a close friendship, and in Jim's ensuing visits to Thailand, he would spend many hours in the doctor's modest home in Mae Sot. During their meetings, which sometimes lasted until the early morning hours, Dr. Singh would teach Jim many things about the Karen. The two men discussed the entire situation in Burma, and how to help its suffering people. There were so many needs—food and medicine for the sick and injured, especially for those in hiding, proper care and education for the children caught in the crossfire, and even Bibles for those who wanted them. Unfortunately, they were all things that cost money— something that neither Jim nor Dr. Singh had.

But if Jim would have his way, the Karen would no longer be a forgotten people. The more he learned about their suffering, the more resolved he became to help shatter the silence about this genocidal war in Asia that no one was talking about.

JIM RETURNED TO China twice in 1996. He made both trips with his brother-in-law, Bob Sweet III, who had also been helping him with the establishment of CSI's United States branch. Both trips, while made with the same intentions, would have very different outcomes.

With Dennis Balcombe's assistance, Jim re-entered China for a second time, armed with a determination to help even more underground church members than his first visit. In the past several months alone, Revival Christian Church had already helped dozens of couriers cross the border into China, and thousands of Bibles and other Christian publications had been successfully delivered into the hands of Chinese Christians who were desperately hungry for God's Word. And yet, despite the success of the Donkeys for Jesus program, still more Bibles were needed by the underground network. Christianity was exploding in China, and the supply of Scriptures that was trickling into the country was nowhere close to fulfilling the demand for them.

Once again, as Jim secretly met with house church leaders to deliver his own contribution of Bibles, the true danger of his mission always loomed in front of him. As he cautiously made an exchange one day in the dining room of a McDonald's restaurant in Tiananmen Square, shoving a duffle bag filled with illegal Bibles underneath a chair, he thought incredulously about the lengths he was forced to go through simply for a few copies of a book. One thing, he knew, was for sure: the Chinese government understood the power of that book and the influence it had on human lives, or else it wouldn't be so adamant in keeping it out of the country.

But the fact still remained that Bible smuggling in China was a serious operation, and if caught, could hold even more serious consequences.

"FORBIDDEN!" IT WAS the only English word that the men who suddenly surrounded Jim and Bob knew how to say.

The unthinkable was happening before Jim's eyes, right in the Beijing airport. He was returning to China for the third time in a matter of months, this time without the help of Dennis Balcombe and Revival Christian Church. He had flown into Beijing with his own supply of Bibles — a decision that now, as he and his brother-in-law stood trapped like terrified deer in headlights, was proving to be an utterly foolish one. But the contents of the bags they carried could very well determine the fate of both their lives, and Jim had to think fast.

"What's forbidden?" he challenged the menacing authorities, instantly slipping into the role of an unsuspecting tourist. "These are just books! I don't see any signs...where does it say '*FORBIDDEN*' in here?"

"*FORBIDDEN!*" the men insisted.

Now knee-deep in the predicament, Jim adamantly demanded to know why he was not allowed to take the harmless "books" into the country. Despite the volley of irate arguments that continued back and forth between them, the men seemed ready to seize the entire supply of Bibles until, with more quick thinking, Jim asked if he could, perhaps, be allowed to take *some* of them into the country.

The new round of negotiations would last for some time, but fortunately, the men were beginning to consider Jim's request. There was a variety of Bibles in his inventory—some that were strictly New Testaments, and some that included maps or concordances. When all was said and done, the men finally granted them permission to keep a few of each type of Bible; the rest were confiscated. After one of the most intimidating moments of his life, Jim left the Beijing airport with about 25 of his Bibles. It certainly wasn't what he had planned, but at least something was better than nothing—especially since he had come such a long way to deliver them.

Getting caught with a "forbidden" stash of Bibles, however, was only the beginning of Jim's troubles. He and Bob left the airport and checked into a hotel, prepared to deliver what precious few Bibles remained in their possession. But unlike the previous trips, something seemed amiss this time. In the days that followed, Jim was unable to make any of his usual contacts to set up the Bible deliveries—and without contacts, the trip couldn't possibly be a success.

And then there was the mysterious phone call. It came from a stranger, someone who was not on the list of Jim's Chinese contacts. The man spoke nearly perfect English, and seemed interested in asking Jim a lot of probing questions about the reason for his stay in China. As strange as the call was, Jim wouldn't fully realize its implications until weeks later.

After two more days of unsuccessful attempts to distribute his Bibles, Jim finally left China. Since assuming his leadership role with CSI USA and learning about the true affliction of persecuted Christians, he was becoming more and more committed to doing whatever he could to help, especially for Chinese Christians. Despite the failure of this last trip — not to mention the confiscation of his Bibles — Jim was determined to go back.

But as it turned out, the Chinese government had other plans. While attempting to return to China just a couple months later, Jim was informed by the Chinese embassy in Washington D.C. that he had been denied access into the country.

After recovering from the initial shock, the news was both frustrating and disappointing. The confiscation of his Bibles in Beijing had clearly been instrumental in raising suspicion about the nature of his visits, and the decision to venture into the country on his own had, without a doubt, been a costly mistake. After the incident at the airport, the mysterious phone call he'd received had likely been from a government employee, someone who was probably gathering information about the foreigner who had been determined to bring contraband across the borders of their homeland. But as discouraging as it was to think about, at least he and Bob had managed to escape the entire escapade with their freedom — and even more importantly, their lives.

It was hard to believe, but Jim, like Dennis Balcombe, had officially joined the ranks of those who were blacklisted from the Communist country. As quickly as it had opened, the door to China had closed on him, perhaps forever. Without being able to personally deliver Bibles and other aid, all that was left for him to do was to pray for those who were suffering — to pray and, by all means, tell anyone who would listen about what was *really* going on in China.

As brief as it had been, his experience with the underground church was certainly not without its merit.

Because of his visits, many Chinese Christians not only had their own copies of the Scriptures, but had also been deeply inspired simply by the presence of a fellow believer who had risked his own life to travel across the world to personally deliver them. While in China, Jim had also helped set up a support program for the families of imprisoned Christians—husbands, wives and children who were not only missing their loved ones but were suffering severe economic hardship because of their absence.

From the moment he set foot on the country's soil, his visits to China had been exhilarating as well as challenging—from navigating his way through a culture so different from his own to meeting others who shared such a fundamentally important part of his life: faith in Jesus Christ. Even when he'd become gravely ill with a mysterious ailment on his second trip, God had seen to his recovery and safe return home to America.

Although he knew that he'd affected many people during his visits, Jim's experiences in China had changed his own life, as well as his commitment to God, in ways that he never would have anticipated. And for as long as he was able, he would make sure that those who were suffering and dying for their faith in China would never be a forgotten people, either.

Parting Ways

The name "Christian Freedom International" captures what we do because we want people to live for their faith, and for them to be free. We're not about representing martyrs, we're about getting people free. We want you to live for your faith, not die for it...we think that you're more effective if you're healthy and you have freedom to evangelize, so we're about promoting freedom.

Jim Jacobson

"DO SMALL THINGS *with great love.*" The quotation from the late Mother Teresa stretched across five feet of a classroom wall in an Aurora, Colorado elementary school. Its simplistic and yet profound meaning was enough to move a group of fifth grade students into action the day they learned about the slave trade in Sudan.

They had just finished a unit study about the Civil War, and, naively, had thought that slavery was a thing of the past. But when their teacher read a newspaper article to them about what was going on in the African country, they were collectively moved to tears. *No one,* they thought, has the right to own another person.

With a little Internet research, the students learned about a slave redemption program pioneered by a humanitarian organization called Christian Solidarity International. CSI was intensely active in buying back the freedom of Sudanese slaves, and another organization, the American Anti-Slavery Group in Boston, Massachusetts, was helping to raise money for CSI's redemption efforts.

Christian Solidarity International was successfully redeeming those caught in the mire of slavery for an amount of just $50 each. Completely intrigued with the entire abolitionist movement, the students began to wonder if perhaps they, too, could buy back a slave's freedom. They launched an impassioned awareness and fundraising campaign, doing everything from writing letters to celebrities and government leaders to raising money with lemonade stands and toy sales. As their cause began to receive nationwide publicity, individual and corporate donations began pouring in from around the country. For every $50 raised, the students added another paper cutout of a freed slave to their classroom wall.

They were not the only ones infuriated by the situation in Sudan. Dozens of groups, organizations and individuals alike were following suit with their own redemption efforts, and as tens of thousands of American dollars were raised, the momentum continued to grow. The funds were enough to allow CSI's John Eibner to travel to Sudan every two months on redemption expeditions, setting free hundreds of slaves at a time.

But despite the overwhelming support for the cause, trouble was brewing for Christian Solidarity International. The lack of uniformity among its branch offices had been causing internal strife for months; now, in the wake of bitter disputes and accusations, several international offices, including the ones in Great Britain, Australia and Germany, had already broken away from the organization.

With Karen by his side, Jim traveled to Switzerland for a third — and what would be his last — CSI conference in the fall of 1997. He, too, had been raising money for slave redemption, and he came to the conference with another important piece of news: CSI USA had fulfilled its two-year obligation to become a self-sufficient organization.

It had been a long journey, compounded by the fact that CSI USA had experienced its own share of difficulties and policy disputes with the Swiss. There had been many occasions when the monthly seed money promised by CSI headquarters never materialized, and Jim often struggled just to pay his staff salaries without it. But now it was official — CSI USA was generating its own income, and was finally operating without the financial help of the Swiss.

By early 1998, however, Jim and the CSI USA board of directors had come to a decision: they would break away from Christian Solidarity International altogether and form their own organization.

The decision had been a long time in coming; nevertheless, it was something that almost seemed necessary. Despite the unique organizational structure of each CSI affiliate branch, the Swiss had been attempting to force all international offices to comply with their own regulations — a matter that had become an unending source of conflict. The all-consuming slave redemption program was another contentious issue, as well.

For months Jim had relied solely on Swiss reports and information about the crisis in Sudan, and although the U.S. branch had no humanitarian programs of its own being conducted in the region, it was still expected to direct all of its fundraising efforts towards slave redemption. Jim was as outraged as everyone else at the news that was being reported about the slave trade, but the fact was that he had already personally witnessed the severity of Christian persecution in other countries. Help was unquestionably needed in Sudan, but to Jim, it was just as important that aid, advocacy and funds were distributed across the world however—and whenever—they were needed.

Mike Farris would remain on the new organization's board of directors, as well as Ambassador Faith Whittlesey. In the three years since Jim had been the executive director of CSI USA, together they had recruited other board members who were just as passionate about the cause of Christian persecution as they were: Paul Behrens, a former Marine Corps Lieutenant; Robert Reilly, a former head of Voice of America, an international radio broadcasting network; George Dunlop, Principal Deputy Assistant Secretary for the U.S. Army Corps of Engineers; Oklahoma Senator Don Nickles; Erik Prince, a former Navy SEAL officer; and eventually Nathaniel Moffat, a businessman and former Assistant to the Director of the Executive Branch Liaison with the Heritage Foundation, a Washington, D.C.-based think tank.

With the decision final, one of the first tasks at hand was to select a new name for the organization. They kicked around several options, until "Christian Freedom International" (CFI) finally seemed most appropriate for a nonprofit committed to defending the religious rights of persecuted Christians around the world.

Thailand
March, 1998

FROM THEIR CONCRETE bunker in the Huay Kaloke refugee camp, two Karen sisters prayed fearfully as they listened to the sound of nearby soldiers setting bamboo huts on fire.

It was not the first time the camp had been attacked by enemy troops. Huay Kaloke had suffered a similar widespread attack just a year earlier, when the vicious rampage of Burmese troops nearly leveled the camp to the ground. The Thai army had promised that an attack of such magnitude would never occur again, and the camp was rebuilt on the same location by the Moei River.

Now the Burmese soldiers were back.

As he crouched with his wife and daughters in the dark, cramped pit, Kyaw Zwa also listened to the dreaded thunder of rocket-propelled grenades and assault rifles over his head. Twenty years earlier, he'd been a soldier for the Karen National Union before losing his left leg in combat; now, he and his family were struggling for survival in a refugee camp.

It had been shortly after midnight when he spotted Burmese soldiers setting fire to the Baptist church they attended, just 30 yards from their home. Fearing that their house would be next to go up in flames, he quickly ordered his family out of their hut and into the nearby makeshift bunker, an eight-foot hole in the ground he'd dug in anticipation of an enemy attack. Now, in the midst of the din above them, they could hear the soldiers shouting at fellow refugees, demanding to know if they were Buddhist or Christian.

The family's home was engulfed in flames just moments later, and a raging heat suddenly flooded the bunker. The sisters leapt out of the pit, screaming frantically as fire quickly consumed their clothing. Neighbors tried to stop them long enough to peel the garments from their skin, but their efforts were to no avail.

Initial reports of the attack on Huay Kaloke suggested that as many as 50 armed soldiers entered the camp, systematically setting fire to homes and shooting at people as they fled into the surrounding fields. In the early morning hours following the incident, at least 30 refugees were treated for gunshot, shrapnel and fire injuries at a Mae Sot hospital. Kyaw Zwa and his family were numbered among the burn victims, with his wife suffering from severe burns on her back, arms and face. Because he had been shielded by his family on the bottom of the pit, Kyaw Zwa survived the attack with only minor burns on his scalp, hands and back. His daughters, however, would not be so fortunate; both girls subsequently died from their injuries.

It was an unbearable loss for the man who'd once fought so valiantly for his country. As his family prepared for bed just hours before the attack, Kyaw Zwa overheard his older daughter in prayer, thanking God for the family's bamboo hut in the camp at a time when many of their fellow Karen were homeless and forced to sleep under trees in the jungle. After the attack began, both daughters had adamantly insisted that, because of his disability, their father should be first to enter the bunker, and they would protect him by acting as a shield on the top.

Now both girls were gone, and Kyaw Zwa would never stop mournfully thinking that *he* should have been the one at the top of the bunker, protecting his children from the violent attack. To the world around them, they were just two more casualties in a violent and senseless assault on a group of homeless refugees. But to their heartbroken father, their deaths would always be a reminder of the incessant war that seemed destined to wipe his people — Christians first — from the face of the earth.

JIM TRAVELED TO Burma several days after the Huay Kaloke attack.

He had been working closely with Drs. Panter and Singh in their quest to help the Karen, and the summer of 1998 was only the beginning of his ongoing work in the region. On this trip, Jim would enter Burma through Thailand, although he had no visa with which to legally enter the country. Once across the border, he would be escorted over the Moei River to the Karen military base in the small village of Tennutah.

The trip was unquestionably risky. Although the base was located just a few miles from the docking point in Thailand, enemy troops had recently been spotted in the region. As he would do on many other occasions, Jim placed his life into the hands of the Karen guerillas that would escort him to his destination. If caught by the Burmese, the consequences could be deadly.

The group docked in Burma before starting the long trek up a narrow path through the jungle. Saw Pothawda, a doctor and former Karen soldier who was also Jim's guide on the trip, warned Jim to avoid landmines by carefully staying on the path in front of him.

After safely reaching the base, Jim was introduced to the camp's general before being led to a dilapidated, makeshift hospital.

Win Oo, a Buddhist Karen soldier who had recently stepped on a landmine, was smoking a cigarette as he reclined on a bamboo platform in the hospital. As flies crawled across his bandages, he explained to Jim that Burmese soldiers had attempted to recruit him into their army, with the argument that the Karen National Union was only led by a group of self-serving Christians. Karen Christians, he'd been told, were the "closed-eye people" because they closed their eyes when they prayed, as opposed to Buddhists who were "open-eyed," and therefore knew much more than the "closed-eye" people.

As he studied the bleak hospital surroundings while interviewing the young soldier, the urgency of the need before him was becoming more and more clear to Jim. The dense jungle was home to hundreds of Karen men, women and children, and far too many of them were suffering without access to some kind of medicine or medical care. Skirting the landmines placed in their path by the Burmese army had become a way of life for refugees, and many of them—including Karen soldiers—were living with the painful cost of having stepped on the deadly weapons. The Karen were in desperate need of as much medical help as possible, and somehow Jim intended to get it for them.

He returned to the United States, and shared an important vision with CFI's donors in the next issue of the organization's newsletter. With the help of Dr. Singh, the plan was to construct a medical facility right in the Burmese jungle, where sick or wounded refugees would not just be able to be receive crucial medical care, but would be treated with Christian love and respect. Staffed by trained, indigenous medical personnel, "Freedom Hospital" would not only help save lives, but would give hope to persecuted refugees.

With no electricity, running water, or any type of modern medical equipment, Freedom Hospital was not much to speak of by American standards. Wooden platforms were used as beds and operations were performed on bamboo tables, but the clinic's very existence would soon become pivotal in the survival of dozens of refugees who suffered from diarrhea, typhoid, dysentery, malaria, measles, tuberculosis and uterine infections, as well as landmine injuries. CFI also established a "backpack medic" program, where groups of trained Karen workers would strap baskets filled with medical supplies onto their backs before venturing into the deepest parts of the jungle. They would travel for miles if necessary, narrowly sidestepping landmines and dodging enemy attacks to deliver medicine and Bibles to fellow refugees who were too sick or injured to travel to Freedom Hospital for treatment.

As the organization gained support for its efforts, its medical programs in Burma would become the cornerstone of its humanitarian work. But in the weeks immediately after its official separation from Christian Solidarity International, CFI had yet another decision to make. The organization still possessed thousands of dollars that had been earmarked for slave redemption in Sudan, and it seemed both senseless and tragic to not use the funds for their intended purpose.

For reasons that were unbeknownst to Jim, CSI had never granted him permission to travel to Sudan on redemption expeditions. Now, as president of his own organization, Jim was not only determined to help free

as many slaves as possible, but to personally do it himself.

There was just one problem. The truth he was
about to uncover would change the way he thought
about the Sudanese slave trade forever.

The Redemption Conspiracy

Slavery in Sudan was a major fundraiser. This issue, more than anything else, was highlighting Christian persecution, because the Arab Muslims in the north were coming down and enslaving the black Christians in the south. Like no other issue, this was just captivating the hearts of Christians in America.

I was told by numerous people that I was going to ruin the issue of religious persecution if I exposed this, so "don't do it." But I remember talking to other ministry leaders, saying, "If you guys continue on this, someday 60 Minutes *or* Dateline *is going to do a special on it, and you're going to be found doing a bad thing. And it's going to hurt everybody." And sure enough, a couple of years later, 60* Minutes *did do an investigative report on this thing. Fortunately, we had exposed something really bad that was taking place and hurting people.*

Jim Jacobson

THE CESSNA CARAVAN—a small, single-engine plane with seating for only a handful of passengers— was the method of transportation that Jim chose for his flight into southern Sudan.

The bush pilot he'd hired to fly them into the region was uneasy about the trip, and with good reason. From the time the plane lifted off the ground in Loki-chokio until it would reach its destination in Sudan, it was of the utmost importance that the aircraft remain as far beneath the radar as possible. If the northern Suda-nese army caught sight of their plane, they would become easy targets for catastrophe.

It was the second time Jim was returning to the country, and he was not alone on the trip—unlike his first visit just a few months earlier, this time he was accompanied by a journalist. As they set out on a new quest to free as many slaves as they could, both men would realize what Jim had already begun to fear: something was terribly wrong with the slave redemption movement in Sudan.

SINCE THE ARRIVAL of its independence in 1955, Sudan had spent nearly all of the subsequent decades gripped in the violence and devastation of a longstanding war with itself. By the late 1990s, civil war had caused the deaths of nearly two million people, with the displacement of millions more. As the Muslim north remained intent on dominating the Christian south, the atrocities committed in the name of religion throughout the years would brand the crisis as one of the worst humanitarian disasters in history.

In 1983, a rebellion was triggered after the Islamic government's failed attempt to transfer southern battalions to the north, thereby removing the south's ability

Jim with Pet Dog Lady

University of Michigan Graduation Ceremony, 1986

Jim and Karen Jacobson at White House
Christmas Party, 1987

Jim with Ronald and Nancy Reagan

Jim with Nephew Ben at White House July 4th Celebration

Jim with Bob Sweet III and Ambassador Faith Whittlesey

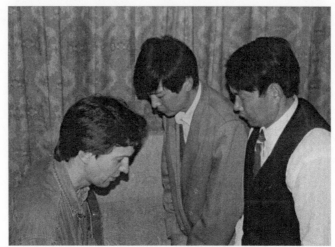

Jim Praying with Underground Church Pastors in China

Jim in Refugee Camp in Thailand

Jim with SPLA Soldiers, Sudan

Backpack Medics, Burma

Jim at Target Practice with KNU

Jim at CFI Freedom Clinic, Burma

to resist. Instead, the rebels fled to Ethiopia, where they were able to organize and militarily equip themselves into a strong force that, under the leadership of career soldier John Garang, would become known as the Sudan People's Liberation Army (SPLA). Although the faction was composed largely of Christians, other non-Arab ethnic groups who shared the initial vision of a democratic Sudan would join its ranks. And as they gained the backing of neighboring countries such as Libya, Uganda and Ethiopia, the SPLA soon controlled a majority of the country's southern regions.

Equipped with cash raised by American donors, Jim traveled to Nairobi in the summer of 1998, intent on finding the SPLA's office and anyone who would be willing to help him enter Sudan. For years he had listened to reports about the slave trade and claims of successful redemptions, and at long last, he was finally going to participate in the experience for himself. Jim had no idea how the entire process worked, but what he did know was that he wouldn't be able to do anything without a reliable contact in the region.

His "reliable contact" was a man named Manase Lomole Waya, a Christian and SPLA soldier who agreed to help escort him into Sudan. Like many other Christians, Manase had endured his own share of persecution by the Islamic government. After his acceptance into Juba University as a young man, Manase had been ordered to convert to Islam or he wouldn't be permitted to enroll in the school. Despite his longtime dream of attending college, Manase chose instead to remain a Christian; in retaliation, the government once again warned him to convert or face execution. After being forced into hiding along with other refugees, he finally joined the rebel movement in the south to help fight the repressive government that had caused so much pain and suffering for his people.

Jim soon became friends with Manase; it was a relationship that would serve him well in the coming months. After journeying into Sudan, Manase helped him arrange a meeting with a slave trader, who negotiated with Muslim masters in the north and arranged for the transport of slaves to the south. As the transaction took place under the shade of a tree, Jim suddenly had questions about the group of bedraggled slaves before him. How did they survive the 400-mile walk from the north? And what would happen to them, or where would they go, after their release? His translated questions directed to the crowd didn't seem to yield any satisfying answers.

Jim purchased the freedom of 13 slaves, certain that the knowledge of their liberation would cause some kind of joyous reaction in those who had been set free. The response to the news of their redemption, however, was completely to the contrary. Instead of grateful jubilation, the slaves seemed completely lifeless—there were no smiles or hugs, no thank-yous of any kind. As he watched the strange scene, a nagging doubt began to creep into his mind. For all he knew, these people could have simply been rounded up from the nearest village and forced to play the role of slaves.

Before his first trip to Sudan was over, Jim also traveled to several remote villages and spoke with natives who claimed to be former slaves, people who still carried scars from the brutal beatings they'd received while in captivity. Although his interviews confirmed the belief that slavery did, indeed, exist in southern Sudan, the questions that were irking his conscience had become too great to ignore.

Jim returned to the United States, where the redemption movement was showing no signs of waning
support. But even as donations continued flooding in,
and in the midst of reports claiming that thousands of
slaves were being set free at once, Jim began receiving
disturbing reports about something else: certain fraudulent redemptions were actually encouraging the slave
trade. The process also appeared to be a vicious, greedy
cycle — slave raiders would take the money earned by
redemptions to purchase more guns and subsequently
gather more hostages in village raids, and owners benefited from the sale of their slaves to the traders, who
were also paid to transport slaves back to their destination in the south. The entire thing was a giant breeding
ground for corruption, and to make matters worse, Jim
feared that the best of the international community's
intentions had become the origin of something gone
horribly awry.

When a journalist named Richard Miniter contacted Jim about his experiences in Sudan, Jim didn't
hesitate to share his concerns with him. Richard had
developed an interest in writing an article about the
slave trade, and when he suggested tagging along on
subsequent trips to Sudan to document the redemption
process, Jim agreed.

The Reverend Larry Andrews, a local Virginia official and Jim's colleague on the Warren County Board of
Supervisors, was also interested in joining Jim on the
trip. With Jim's help, Larry had gathered donated pencils and notebooks — just a few of the supplies they
planned to bring to Africa — to deliver to the Dinka
children they would visit on the trip.

And there was something else Jim brought —
something that, in his opinion, was just as important as

the ton of food and medical supplies that had been loaded onto the small aircraft: his digital camera. Documenting the true nature of slave redemption, or even bringing desperately needed aid to the Dinkas, wasn't all that Jim wanted to accomplish on the excursion. If other abuses were going on against Christians anywhere at all in Sudan, he intended to return to America with as much hard proof as possible.

JIM'S PLANE LANDED safely in Sudan, just in time for the slave trader's arrival.

Word had spread throughout nearby villages that a "delivery" from the north was about to be made, and as a table was set up underneath the area's lone tree, a throng of desperate parents quickly surrounded Jim. Dozens of mothers and fathers looked on into the small crowd of slaves, hoping against hope for the miraculous chance to redeem their long lost children. A man known to Jim only as "Bol's father" waited anxiously nearby, praying for the return of his 10-year-old son who'd been sold into slavery two years earlier.

Over the transaction table, the trader announced that he had come to the meeting with only 12 slaves, although Jim was prepared to purchase as many as 50. The northern Islamic army often made it difficult for him to bring more, the trader explained. Though the man was motivated by profit as much as compassion, Jim knew that the trader truly did risk his own safety each time he transported slaves to the south. If captured by the Islamic army, he could very well face his own imprisonment, beating, or even execution.

Jim purchased the freedom of all 12 slaves, glad to realize that one young boy in the group was, in fact, "Bol," the long-lost son of the man who'd been waiting so expectantly behind him. Even in the midst of the boy's joyous reunion with his father, the heartbroken disappointment of the other parents in the crowd was not lost on Jim.

The trader promised to return north to collect more slaves, so Jim left enough money with the translator to purchase the freedom of several dozen more people. The suffering and misery in Sudan was overwhelming, and he knew the memories would stay with him for a long time to come.

AS IF THE devastation of poverty and the inhumanity of slavery weren't enough, the untold damage caused by hundreds of landmines throughout the country was yet another destructive force in Sudan.

Jim knew firsthand about the deadly consequences of minefields. He and his companions spent much of their time traveling in vehicles that were led by teams of men walking cautiously in front of them, searching the ground for explosives. But the men had no detectors to aid them in their search, and more than once Jim had prayed fervently to God that they wouldn't inadvertently set one off. On one occasion, a truck that had been traveling in front of them ran over a mine, killing everyone in the vehicle. It had been a frighteningly close call, and to Jim, the incident was a grave reminder not only of God's divine protection during his travels, but of just how quickly life could change in an instant.

It was the minefields that made travel so difficult for many Dinka villagers. Well aware of the necessity of a good education if they were ever to break out of the ruthless cycle of poverty, the Dinkas had been attempting to build a brick schoolhouse for their children for months. But getting supplies for the construction work had been slow at best, if for nothing other than the sheer difficulty of getting around the minefields that surrounded their village.

With the help of Manase Lomole Waya, Jim and his group navigated their way through roads littered with landmine-destroyed trucks to deliver the supplies they'd brought for their fellow Christians in the Dinka village. They came bringing food, antibiotics and vitamins, as well as the donated school supplies for the children, whose eyes lit up when they saw the fresh, clean notebooks and new, unused pencils.

Larry Andrews, a long-time farmer back in his rural home in Virginia, also gave the villagers helpful farming advice, and even inspected an old, disabled tractor that had been rendered useless after hitting a landmine. If the ravages of war would simply go away, the Dinkas would be free to not only invest in their children with the construction of a schoolhouse, but they would be able to grow enough food to feed the entire country on the rich, fertile soil that surrounded them.

A conversation with two Dinka soldiers brought unsettling news. The men informed Jim and Larry that they had recently been the victims of what was believed to be a chemical weapons attack by the Islamic militia, just outside the city of Juba. An enemy bomber had been spotted dropping a mysterious canister over the area, and many nearby Dinkas suffocated and died after the canister exploded. Although there was no physical evidence, the incident seemed to carry all the implications of a mustard gas attack.

Jim was already aware of intelligence reports indicating that, just months earlier, the United States bombed a factory in Sudan that had allegedly been manufacturing chemical weapons. Before they left the village, he promised the Dinkas that CFI would attempt to collect various soil samples that, once tested, would hopefully confirm their suspicions.

The thought that such a cruel weapon would be used against so many innocent people was appalling, but then again, there wasn't much of anything that was surprising Jim anymore.

BY EARLY 1999, Jim's experiences in Sudan were causing him to become more doubtful than ever about slave redemption, especially when he learned about the U.N.'s World Food Program—another humanitarian effort that, ironically, only seemed to encourage the slave trade. After the United Nations routinely asked permission from the Islamic government to make scheduled airlifts of food and medical supplies into various impoverished regions in southern Sudan, government-backed raiders would swoop into the areas just in time to seize the shipments, as well as a new round of local villagers to carry away into the vicious cycle of slavery.

Jim and Rich Miniter would witness for themselves the devastating effects of slave raids on their next trip to the region.

They had barely stepped off the plane when several local villagers rushed up to them, carrying an elderly woman. Hundreds of raiders just attacked their village of Akoch, they explained frantically, and as dozens of people were being killed or carried away as slaves, their grandmother had been viciously slashed by a horseman. She was gravely ill, and could they fly her to the hospital in Lokichokio, a U.N. settlement just inside the Kenya/Sudan border?

Jim and Rich stared in horror at the woman's head wound—a gash deep enough to see the yellow membrane surrounding her brain. As the family laid the woman underneath the plane's wing, the pilot radioed the U.N. compound for help. The woman was in serious need of medical attention, but somehow, Jim knew what the answer would be, even before it came.

"Does she have a valid passport and visa to travel into Kenya?" the U.N. official on the other end of the radio asked them.

"No, she doesn't have either," Jim answered.

"Then the hospital is full," the voice replied.

Astonished at the response, the family stared in confusion into the half-empty plane. Jim knew they could never understand the politics of the situation—that waiting on the other side of the border were apathetic bureaucrats who, even if they did make the flight into Kenya, would simply force them to turn around and return the dying woman to the war zone she'd come from.

Jim left the family with a variety of medical supplies, knowing there was not much else he could do for her. He would never learn the fate of Anchor Ring, the woman whose life had taken such a sudden, heartbreaking turn even as her grandchildren were likely being snatched away into cruel, inhuman captivity. He could only rest in the fact that, in that tragic moment in time, her fragile life was in the hands of God.

THE CENSUS AMONG the Dinkas seemed to be unanimous: no one believed in redemption as a solution to the problem of slavery.

In the days following the attack on Akoch, Jim and Rich spoke with many of the village residents, including its executive chief. Redemption encourages the raiders, they said. To pay the men who killed your father and stole your brother only puts out an invitation for them to return.

At one villager's suggestion, Rich located and interviewed another man who'd once been held captive following a previous raid on Akoch. After a day of marching in captivity across the desert, the man managed to escape before sunrise, hiding for several hours until the raiders finally departed from the area. With his hands still tied behind his back, he made the long walk home to find his wife and family missing, his hut burned, and all his cattle gone. Slave redemption is bad, he said simply when Rich asked him about the matter. The raiders are doing terrible things to put money in their pockets, and he didn't understand why anyone would give it to them.

IF THEIR CONVERSATIONS with the Dinkas weren't enough to confirm Jim's long-standing reservations, his next attempt at redemption would prove to be another nail in the coffin.

Nyamlell, a large settlement fifty miles north of the Bahr al Arab River in southern Sudan, was one of the most popular redemption sites covered by the United States media. It was also the location where Jim hoped to purchase the freedom of another group of slaves—until he got a call from the Sudanese Relief and Rehabilitation Association (SRRA), the humanitarian wing of the SPLA.

Accompanied by Rich Miniter, Jim met the SRRA officials in their branch office in Lokichokio, Kenya. After several minutes of small talk, Jim was finally questioned about his intended transaction in Nyamlell: How much money did he have for the redemption?

Jim's answer of $4,000 seemed to please the officials, who promptly informed him that 40 children were waiting to be redeemed. As Jim quickly did the math, he realized that, at that rate, he would be paying $100 per slave. Don't other groups pay only $50 per slave? he asked the men. No, they replied, everyone pays $100. When Jim asked about the $50 redemption price that he knew was routinely set for Christian Solidarity International, he was told that CSI was an exception because the organization purchased slaves in much larger quantities.

The ruse was becoming more obvious by the minute, but Jim continued to play along. Two SRRA officials insisted on accompanying Jim and Rich on the ride to Nyamlell, where a local commissioner was waiting as the plane touched down on the dirt runway.

The commissioner, who refused to make eye contact with either of the SRRA officials, adamantly told the men that he needed to speak privately with the two Americans. A guard with an AK-47 kept the officials at bay as the commissioner escorted Jim and Rich to a nearby compound. Over an offering of tea, he admitted to Jim and Rich that there were no slaves to be redeemed in Nyamlell.

The situation was becoming even more suspicious. Didn't the SRRA contact their village the previous day and learn that there were 40 slave children to be redeemed? Jim asked. No, the commissioner repeated. There were *no* slaves in Nyamlell.

As they returned to the airstrip, one of the SRRA officials informed Jim that he had just located a slave trader with 10 children to redeem. The announcement seemed to anger the commissioner, who suddenly pulled Jim out of hearing range of the officials and insisted that he leave immediately. The children were not slaves, he said, but were in fact children from a nearby village. We do not want you to do this, he pleaded with Jim fervently. We are Christians...and we do not want the world to turn its face from us.

We do not want the world to turn its face from us. The commissioner's frank honesty would eventually cost him his job, but the incident was more than enough to substantiate Jim's beliefs about the fraudulent nature of slave redemption. After months of being absorbed in the heartrending nightmare that was plaguing the country, Jim finally came to an agonizing decision: he would withdraw CFI's support of the slave redemption movement. In a country as poor as Sudan, the monetary incentives behind the entire process could never serve as anything other than a wide-open door to greed and dishonesty. And although the practice had unquestionably saved the lives of many legitimate slaves over the years, the widespread suffering it was causing to thousands more innocent people could never justify its existence.

The more he thought about it, the more Jim realized the necessity of speaking out about his firsthand knowledge of slave redemption. As deeply involved as the Christian community had become in the matter, everyone certainly needed to know — or, at least, would appreciate knowing — all that he knew, or so he thought.

He had no idea how wrong he was.

Dangerous Faith

It was probably the most dangerous time I've ever had in Burma.

The SPDC knew that I was there, and they were coming to get us. What started out to be a two-day trip to visit one of our Freedom Hospitals turned out to be about a 14-day trip, just trying to outflank the SPDC. We were exhausted because we had to keep moving at night and then hide during the day, and we got into a situation where we were mortared. The Karen have a routine where you'd put your hand on the back of the next guy to distance yourself, so when the mortars popped in, everyone wouldn't get killed. We were in the jungle, it was pitch black, and the only way to move ahead was to hang onto the guy in front of you. And so we had this long human train, hour after hour in total darkness.

We were delayed because Mimi, Dr. Singh's daughter, was with us on the trip. She got exhausted to the point where they had to put in an IV, because she was going to die. We had to carry her on a bamboo stretcher, and it delayed us by about three hours to get to the road crossing. But we later found out that there were over 100 SPDC soldiers waiting to take us out at the crossing. Since we were so delayed, they thought we weren't coming, and they went away.

It was God's hand, once again, that really made all the difference in that particular mission.

Jim Jacobson

Iran
January, 1997

THE SECRET COULD cost him his life.

As he stepped into the baptismal pool, Hamid[1] was keenly aware of the potential consequences of what he was about to do. Both religious law and the civil code of the land warranted death as the appropriate punishment for conversion in Iran. Although many non-Muslims were free to practice their faith, converts were a different story altogether. Conversion to Christianity was indisputably viewed as a "crime against God," and Hamid had personally seen many Christians hanged in the street for their disloyalty to the Muslim faith.

Now, once a loyal Muslim, he was about to become a "disloyal" convert himself.

As an electrical systems manager with the National Oil Company, Hamid's salary earned him about $225 per month, with an additional $6,000 to $10,000 a year for special projects—a rather comfortable income for an average citizen in Iran. But Hamid knew his middle-class life couldn't save him from the danger of being a converted Christian. For months after his baptism, his

---

[1] Name changed for privacy.

life was shrouded under a veil of secrecy, fear, and nightmares of the Islamic police.

In January 1998, everything began unraveling right before his eyes.

After the police raided a prayer service he was attending one evening, Hamid was arrested and subsequently sent home after a long interrogation. But Hamid knew trouble was brewing when he was arrested again just one month later; the police, it seemed, were surely building a case against him.

As the news of his arrest began to spread, things quickly went from bad to worse. His supervisor unapologetically informed him that infidels were not wanted at the National Oil Company, and Hamid was terminated from his job. School had become nothing but a place of torment for his 18-year-old daughter, who was routinely subjected to verbal and physical abuse from fellow students while teachers stood by and watched the harassment approvingly. Islamic militants told Hamid's wife, who had also been secretly baptized, that she should be killed because she didn't belong in such a "clean society." As her home-based sewing business — the only other source of income they had — quickly began to fail, Hamid and his family found themselves relying on close relatives for financial help.

When an old friend, who was also an employee at the Islamic court, warned Hamid that his re-arrest was imminent, he hurriedly sold his family's belongings before packing what was left into a single suitcase. On June 28, 1999, two years after he had given his life to Christ, a panic-stricken Hamid furtively led his wife and children onto a bus that would take them to the large city of Tabriz.

But a new ordeal was just around the corner...

THE LETTER WAS four pages long, and it was one of the most difficult things that Jim would ever have to write.

The letter was informing 6,000 donors of a very important decision: Christian Freedom International would no longer support the practice of slave redemption in Sudan.

Jim explained that, although the decision had been "painful," it was one that now reflected his firm beliefs that redemption fueled not only Sudan's slave trade, but the country's entire civil war. The initial objective for humanitarian groups, including his own, had simply been to document the appalling atrocities surrounding the slave trade and to raise international awareness of them. Instead, the overwhelming financial support of Western Christians and organizations had, ironically, only proved to be hurting the cause of slavery more than it was helping.

In the letter, Jim also explained that, although CFI was no longer actively redeeming Sudanese slaves, many other important programs were still being conducted in the region. To that end, each donor had the option of either redirecting their funds towards CFI's other humanitarian projects or have the money returned to them in the form of a refund.

The reaction to the news that CFI was no longer supporting what had become such an all-consuming cause was spreading like poison. As Christian Freedom International refunded nearly $12,000 to disgruntled donors in the weeks following the mailing of Jim's letter, his decision to speak out was inflicting repercussions in ways that he never would have imagined. As his interviews and articles condemning slave redemption began to appear in newspapers and magazines such as *The Denver Post*, *The Washington Times*, *Christianity Today* and *The Atlantic Monthly*, Jim suddenly, strangely, found himself "uninvited" to events in evangelical circles he'd been so widely accepted in just months before. And in spite of his frankness about the situation with his donors, including the refund policy established for slave redemption funds, financial support for CFI had dropped sharply. The notion that so many Christians would be hostile to the truth about such a crucial matter was puzzling, but Jim also knew that slave redemption had become one of the most trendy—and powerful—fundraisers of the day. For someone, anyone, to challenge its validity was almost unthinkable at the time.

Jim had many ideas about how to alleviate the problem of fraudulent redemptions—from putting slave traders on salary to organizing an "underground railroad" system—and didn't hesitate to continue voicing his opinions about them. But even with the controversy that Jim's outspokenness was causing on American soil, something more disturbing was going on in Sudan. As a consequence for exposing the widespread fraud associated with slave redemption, the SPLA had begun issuing thinly veiled threats against him. The rebel group that had once helped him provide food, medicine, school supplies and Bibles to their own impoverished civilians was now implying that his safety would no longer be "guaranteed" if he returned to Sudan. Even worse, Jim would later learn that he had become a most unwelcome target in certain rebel-controlled territories. The message was loud and clear: if he set foot in the country again, he would likely be killed.

They were warnings that Jim did not intend to take lightly. Things were undoubtedly changing in Sudan, especially since the SPLA had begun pressuring other humanitarian groups in the region, demanding that they accept newly imposed conditions or get out of the country altogether. The SPLA was insisting, among other things, that nonprofit organizations make their vehicles available for their use—a precarious situation that would not only jeopardize the neutrality of the organizations, but would put their workers directly in harm's way by making them targets in the unrelenting civil war. Many charities, including CARE, Save the Children and World Vision, refused to comply with the rebels' demands and also withdrew from the region.

In time, Jim would be proven correct in his findings about the corruption that plagued the slave redemption movement, even as Christian Solidarity International came under close scrutiny about its many claims of successful redemptions and its own affiliation with the SPLA. Although Jim himself knew he would not return to the country for a long time, if ever, he still cared deeply about the thousands of people who were suffering under the weight of persecution and poverty in Sudan. With Manase Lomole Waya's help, CFI continued to ship clothing and other relief aid into the country, and even donated funds to establish vocational schools. Jim would not be there to see it, but as CFI's seeds blossomed into fruitful ministries in the years to come, God's faithful provision for His people in war-torn Sudan would affect an untold amount of people for all of eternity.

BY THE SUMMER of 2001, Jim had lost count of his trips overseas to Burma. He was traveling to the country so frequently—nearly every other month, for days at a time—that he'd stopped taking his malaria prescription out of fear that its prolonged use would damage his kidneys.

As CFI rebounded from the slave redemption controversy, Jim was busier than ever working in jungles and refugee camps for a people whose suffering only seemed to be intensifying. The truth was that he loved spending time with the Karen, and even joined them to mourn the death of Dr. Singh, who had passed away after a massive heart attack while on a backpack medic run in the jungle in early 1999. His burning desire and enthusiasm to help Burma's persecuted Christians had contagiously passed on to friends, family and business acquaintances, and his wife and children even accompanied him on a two-month trip to the country in the summer of 2001. He remained a tireless advocate for the Karen and Karenni people, determined to not only continue the vision of the late Dr. Singh but to make known to the entire world the abject suffering of so many of Burma's refugees.

He had developed many other contacts and friendships in the course of his work in Burma, from KNU generals and soldiers to Dr. Singh's oldest daughter, Mimi, who had selflessly chosen to carry on the work of her father. Each and every one of them had personally witnessed or experienced the horrors of life in Burma, and for most of them, their Christian faith had only been strengthened as a result of such relentless persecution. Each carefully cultivated relationship enhanced CFI's credibility in the region, and gave Jim access to opportunities he wouldn't have necessarily had without them. But despite his growing list of allies, the danger

117

of a deadly encounter with enemy troops continued to loom over his shoulder like an ominous shadow.

As CFI's donor base regained its strength, more funds were added to humanitarian programs in Burma. The organization built additional Freedom Hospitals, as well as orphanages and Bible schools in several refugee camps. And as more and more refugees found themselves cut off from desperately needed medical aid in their hiding places deep within the jungle, the backpack medic program continued to be one of CFI's most critical methods of helping the persecuted.

Although many lives were being taken by the endless civil war, malaria was the region's biggest killer. It was a treatable disease, but lifesaving drugs were hard to come by in Burma—so difficult, in fact, that it was actually harder to smuggle them *into* the country than it was to smuggle illegal narcotics *out*. CFI's medical operatives routinely managed to bypass several checkpoints in Thailand and slip boxes of medicine past the border, where they would be placed on a riverboat and sent up the Moei River. On the occasions when Jim accompanied the boat shipment, he hid underneath a tarp to avoid SPDC snipers in the hills above the river.

When the boat had safely reached KNU headquarters, the boxes were unloaded and carried across a stream to the other side of the compound, where they were dropped off at a Freedom Hospital. Although some medicine remained at the facility, most of it would fill the bags of the medics who traveled into the jungle to locate sick and injured villagers.

The "killing season" was yet another problem for refugees in Burma. It was the time of year when the jungle's steep trails dried out, the streams ran low, and it was easier for enemy troops to locate those in hiding.

As SPDC soldiers ravaged entire villages in the jungles, setting fire to everything in their path, CFI's Freedom Hospitals were seldom spared from destruction. But for every hospital that was burned to the ground, a new one was faithfully constructed to take its place.

As CFI's work continued, the personal danger to Jim's life never waned. He was a thorn in the SPDC's side, and he knew that his death would be considered as nothing less than a small victory to the enemy. But for every time he crossed into the war zone, Jim's resolve to carry on drove him to a place beyond himself, a place where he would never rest until he'd made a difference for each and every persecuted Christian within his reach.

Van, Turkey
1999

THINGS WERE NOT going well for Hamid and his family since their escape from Iran.

He'd met with three of his cousins — Christians who were also being persecuted for their faith — in Tabriz, where he was introduced to a Kurdish smuggler who promised to get them into Turkey for the sum of $1,250. The trip was unquestionably dangerous, and the smuggler's fee would deplete nearly all of their savings, but to Hamid, it was a risk he was willing to take if it meant freedom was waiting on the other side.

For several days, the group drove through a series of small villages, made their way by foot and on horseback over steep, dark mountain trails, and crept through hills to avoid border patrol searchlights. They finally arrived in Van, Turkey on July 4, 1999, feeling free for the first time in months.

Their first stop was the Van police station, where their elation quickly came to an end. Hamid and his family were told that, as refugees, they were forbidden to work, apply for welfare, break a strict curfew, or leave Van without a travel permit. They were also required to receive asylum from the UNHCR within six months, or be forced to return to Iran. After contacting the UNHCR office in Turkey, Hamid was told that the first available appointment was, incredibly, over two months away.

Still, it was an opportunity to inform someone about the terrible religious persecution they had suffered in Iran. But when they were finally interviewed by a UNHCR caseworker—a French woman who didn't speak their language and communicated only through a translator—Hamid and his family were neither asked about the injustices they suffered as Christians, nor about their basic Christian beliefs. After several rounds of seemingly irrelevant questions, their plea for asylum was rejected.

It was hard to believe, but after everything they had been through in their quest for freedom, the UNHCR's indifference to their predicament could possibly send Hamid's family back to Iran. After four more agonizing months, the appeal for their rejection was set to be held in the Turkish capital of Ankara. Tired, broke and hungry, the family endured a 24-hour bus ride before finally arriving at the UNHCR office. After several long hours of more trivial, meaningless questions asked by UNHCR officials, Hamid's family was given permission to leave.

They received a U.N. form letter in March of 2000. Its contents seemed almost like a death sentence: "*After carefully examining your application in this second review,*

*you have not been found to meet the refugee criteria under
international refugee law. . . .You are therefore not a person
of concern to UNHCR. As a result, we have closed your file
and are unable to assist you."*

HELP WAS JUST on the horizon for the refugee
family from Iran, and it would come from a variety of
sources in the United States.

Nancy Andisheh, a relative of Hamid's who lived
in Phoenix, Arizona, was aware of the dire situation
and had been wiring money to the family in Van. She
had also begun an intense letter-writing campaign to
numerous lawmakers, including Republican Senators
John McCain, Jon Kyl and Arlen Specter, and her insistence finally convinced them to pressure the U.S. State
Department to look into the situation.

Outraged at the UNHCR's inefficiency and moved
by the desperation of Hamid's plight, Jim also did not
hesitate to take on the case. The fight would be difficult, but time was of the essence for an entire family
whose lives were hanging precariously in the balance.
As Jim met with congressional aides and waded
through the red tape of the refugee process, the Immigration and Naturalization Service (INS) finally agreed
to review the case, despite the fact that it had already
been turned down by the UNHCR. To get the process
started, the International Catholic Migration Commission, a nonprofit group funded by a U.S. government
contract, would interview Hamid's family.

Jim accompanied Nancy Andisheh to Turkey to
prepare the family for their interview with the commission—another amazingly difficult process as the refugees waited to receive travel permits to Istanbul. When
they finally reached their destination and the long-

awaited interviews began, the same dismal pattern seemed as if it would repeat itself as commission officials began yet another line of strangely irrelevant questioning.

Fed up with the injustice of the entire situation, Jim continued to pressure the commission officials — even threatening U.S. Congressional action — until, finally, Hamid's family was respectfully asked about the Christian persecution they had suffered in Iran. The interview resulted in a hearing before the INS, where Hamid, his wife, daughters, and two of his cousins were subsequently given permission to travel to the United States.

Sadly, only part of his family would be joining them on the trip, but for Hamid, the granting of asylum was an incredible, long overdue victory. His simple decision to follow Christ several years ago had put his life, and the lives of his entire family, in grave danger while living in Iran; now, after months of suffering and heartache, they were moving to a land where they would be free to worship the One they so faithfully served — without arrest, without ridicule, without imprisonment, and without fear.

Jim was also thankful that Hamid's ordeal was over. But as the family returned to Van to await the documentation that would allow them to travel to the United States, he knew that, for every Christian who somehow managed to escape persecution, there were hundreds more who never would — Christians who would live, suffer, and die for their faith — all over the world.

Hamid's family, Jim knew, were the lucky ones.

Keeping Promises

We had been planning a big conference in Washington D.C., the Christian Freedom International Freedom Conference. We sent invitations out to everyone, and we had a number of senators and congressmen scheduled to speak. When Washington got shut down, we had to cancel the conference. And ever since then, things have really changed overseas in terms of security and the level of persecution, especially in the Islamic world. If they can't get an American, then they'll go after Christians whom they see as proxies for America, because they view Christianity as a Western religion.

The world has become a very, very bad place for Christians since September 11th.

Jim Jacobson

AS PERSECUTION CONTINUED to rise throughout the world, Christian Freedom International's work became more necessary than ever.

Jim and his staff had begun sending Bibles, food and medical supplies to Laos, Bangladesh and Indonesia, other countries where Christians had been suffering for decades. They also developed a microenterprise program, training destitute Christians to hone their artistic skills and produce quality handcraft items for resale in the United States. As dozens of persecuted believers benefited from the profits generated by their handmade bags, furniture, clothing and even toys, CFI's "self-help" venture soon became an effective way for them to generate essential income.

It was of the utmost importance to Jim that every dollar raised by CFI be used for its intended purpose, and many of his trips overseas were spent checking on the development of ongoing projects to ensure that CFI funds were being used appropriately. As a small, grassroots organization that was to be run with nothing less than the highest level of integrity, he knew it was critical to treat the operation as if its every move was under constant scrutiny from the outside world. As CFI continued to gain the trust of its donors, Jim worked hard to make sure that every promise made to them was kept. If, for whatever reason, a project or program could not continue as planned, he was careful to offer refunds to contributors who did not wish to reallocate their donation to another project. Although it was not required by law to make such an offer, CFI's refund policy was just one of the things that had begun to set them apart from other humanitarian organizations in the nonprofit world.

As Jim spent even more time traveling overseas, the daily responsibilities of raising the Jacobson clan continued to fall on his wife, Karen. The demands at home were clearly growing—Karen had also begun homeschooling their four children—even as the demands of CFI's ministry to the persecuted church were growing each day. Jim was at home far less than he would have liked, but he still managed to take advantage of every opportunity to spend as much time with his children as possible. Conversation was an important dynamic in the Jacobson household, and Jim spent hours talking with them about everything from politics to religion. Each moment, while not as great in quantity as it was in quality, was an investment in a family unit that would only continue to strengthen with the passage of time. And as Kierstin, Kelly, James and Joshua Jacobson grew older, they would join their parents in understanding the critical importance of Christian Freedom International's existence. While no one denied missing Jim on his long and frequent travels, both Karen and the children knew that, as they lived free, comfortable lives in the United States of America, millions of fellow Christians around the world were living in harsh poverty and dying for their faith. If missing their husband and father for several months out of the year meant that the suffering of other believers was being relieved in some small way, it was a sacrifice that the Jacobsons were all too willing to make.

AS HIS OWN children were thriving in Front Royal, Virginia, Jim was becoming increasingly concerned about other people's children in Burma.

He was learning a great deal about the lives of Karen youth during his travels to the region, usually while visiting refugee camps and orphanages. The children were bright, eager to learn, and eager to please—and more often than not, their minds were full of haunting, tragic memories that would surely affect them for the rest of their lives. At Jim's urging during one particular visit, they drew pictures of things they had personally witnessed—men and women being beaten and dragged away in captivity, or babies being ruthlessly bashed against rocks by Burmese soldiers.

With the help of caring and generous supporters, CFI's child sponsorship program was already delivering medicine and other supplies to refugee children, including basic necessities such as cooking oil, soap, mosquito repellant, and food items like powdered milk and sugar for their families. In an effort to make a long-term investment in each child's life as well as providing for day-to-day necessities, the program also offered Christian training and educational support. But even for the children who were receiving some kind of care, Jim's heart was burdened by the fact that so many others were being orphaned and lost in the midst of Burma's war. Without help, they were destined to remain dismally trapped in the life of a refugee. Something more had to be done to improve the odds for as many Karen children as possible.

Jim's idea was to build a school, but not just any school would do. What the children needed was a place where they would not only be safe, away from the depressing environment of the refugee camps and orphanages, but a place where, surrounded by loving Christians, they would truly have a second chance at life—a chance to learn, to grow, and most of all, to dream about what their lives could truly be like with the right opportunities.

It was a challenging project, even as the concept began to take shape. The school would be built along the border in Mae Sot, Thailand, with open fields nearby and mountains in the distance. It was an ideal

Dr. Singh's Funeral, January 2000

Construction of CFI Vocational School Cafeteria

CFI Vocational School in Thailand

Jacobson Family with Vocational School Students

KNU Soldiers, Burma

Jim and Karen Jacobson Interview Karen Soldiers, Burma

Woman with Child in Brickyard, Pakistan

Jim with Brickyard Workers, Pakistan

Jim in Bangladesh

Htoo Eh Paw and Family

Sensual Arts Adult Bookstore, Sault Ste. Marie, MI

CFI in former Sensual Arts Adult Bookstore Building, 2008

location, but getting permission from the Thai authorities to build and operate a boarding school for refugee children was just half of a process that would already be an uphill battle. Getting the right paperwork in order could take years, but the lives of too many children were at stake—they needed help now.

With typical urgency and determination, Jim decided to start building. With God's help, he would have to trust that everything else would fall into place at just the right time.

THE MURDER SENT a furious shockwave throughout the United States.

Still reeling from the devastation of the World Trade Center attacks in New York City, the country was horrified at the news that the body of American journalist Daniel Pearl had been found in Karachi, Pakistan.

It was early 2002, and Pearl, a correspondent for the *Wall Street Journal*, had been on location in Pakistan, investigating the case of shoe bomber Richard Reid. His kidnapping at the hands of an Islamic militant group set off a frantic, two-week search for his whereabouts, until his mutilated body was finally found in Karachi. In the days following the brutal murder, two things became painfully clear: Muslim domination was the driving force in Pakistan, and any non-Muslim who was remotely affiliated with the Western world was a target for destruction.

From his own location in Lahore, Pakistan, Jim was also shocked to hear the news of the journalist's death. He had traveled to Pakistan himself to intervene in another asylum case, working with the U.S. Embassy on behalf of a woman who had been desperately trying to escape the country. Another journalist named Doug

Bandow had accompanied Jim on the trip, as he had already done on several other occasions, to help document the complicated process of untangling a minority Christian out of the hands of an Islamic justice system.

Jim did not need to hear the news of Daniel Pearl's death to be reminded of just how dangerous it was to travel in Pakistan. While secretly delivering medical supplies to Christians in a Khyber Pass refugee camp, Jim and his small entourage had been confronted by several Muslim women who had discovered what they were doing and become angered by their presence in the camp. A mob quickly formed as the women began yelling obscenities and throwing objects in their direction. With the irate crowd close behind them, they ran at top speed towards their dilapidated van, praying desperately that it would start. As the engine sputtered to life and they sped away, Jim was overwhelmingly relieved and yet incredulous at how close to death he'd been — again.

With their numbers tallying in at just under two percent of the population, Christians were the largest minority group in Pakistan. But their inequality in an overwhelmingly Muslim society made them routinely susceptible to harassment, thefts, violent attacks, even abduction and forced conversion to Islam. Before his trip was over, Jim would learn for the first time about yet another injustice carried out against Pakistani Christians. When a tour guide told him about the hundreds of Christians who lived as slaves in Muslim-owned brickyards, Jim was immediately intrigued. He had caught a glimpse of several large brickyards as they drove through an area just outside Lahore, and was amazed to learn that many impoverished Christians, after taking out a desperately needed loan from a Muslim source, were forced to work in brickyards when they could not repay the debt. What was worse, days — or months, or even years — of backbreaking labor didn't even begin to repay a fraction of the loan's interest.

Jim insisted on witnessing life inside the brickyards for himself, although the tour guide warned him that visits by Westerners were practically impossible. But after learning that the master was away from the premises at one particular yard, they finally managed to slip in undetected.

It didn't take long to become overwhelmed by the utter squalor that surrounded them.

Entire families worked alongside each other, creating rows of bricks that stretched across acres of land. Astounded by what he was seeing, Jim interviewed dozens of people, many of whom shared the same miserable story: they had been working all their lives in the brickyards to pay off old debts. Some, in fact, were even working to repay the debts of family members from generations past. But one thing was for sure — there was no escaping life in the brickyards. Even if they somehow managed to flee, they would likely be caught and returned.

The longer the slaves talked, the more heartbreaking details continued to unfold. They told Jim that everyone, including children as young as four, were expected to work 12-hour days, six days a week, under the sweltering hot sun in order to meet the brickmaster's quota. Young babies lay in makeshift beds right in the brickyards as their parents worked. For older children, going to school was out of the question.

The work was as dangerous as it was exhausting. Jim was shown the large ovens where the bricks were baked, and was told that, on more than one occasion, slaves had fallen to their deaths into the searing heat. As he walked across the top of an oven himself, Jim felt the material of his hiking boots beginning to melt under his feet.

At the end of each long, grueling day, the slaves retired into a gathering of crudely made shacks right in the brickyard, with barely enough energy to feed themselves whatever meager portions of food were on hand. It was a dreary existence, with virtually no hope of ever getting out, but Jim was moved by the unwavering faith of many of them—and was already thinking of ways to help. As with most of the suffering Christians he'd met on his travels, the "people of the bricks" had long since learned to rely on God, one day—often one hour—at a time, and therefore had a remarkable spirit that would never be broken.

IN JULY 2002, construction workers poured concrete into the foundation of the building that would become the CFI Vocational School in Thailand.

Jim was excited to see the vision finally begin to materialize. The plan was for children aged 13 to 18 to attend the four-year school, where they would learn English, Thai, the Bible, math, science and history, as well as computer and sewing skills. After graduation, students would have the option of pursuing a higher education or entering the job market. Attendance at the vocational school, he knew, would truly make a difference for many refugee children.

But unlike the fast-paced, deadline-oriented construction projects typical in the United States, progress on the building was agonizingly slow. Nothing of that magnitude had ever been built in the region before, and as the months passed, the effects of the workers' inexperience began to show. More than once the project came to a near standstill as they agonized over the smallest of details, ultimately choosing to wait for Jim's next visit and his advice on how to proceed. When he arrived, Jim would tour the construction site, stare at the shell of the vast building, clear up any issues that were causing the delay, and encourage the workers to press on before leaving with the dim hope that things would look differently when he returned.

By the spring of 2003, Jim and Karen had come to a decision: they would move to Thailand until the vocational school was completed. It was something that was far too important for too many children, and at whatever cost, construction *had* to be completed—and soon. It was obvious that Jim's almost constant presence was necessary at the construction site, and if that were to happen, things would move forward much more quickly.

Neither Jim nor Karen had ever lived outside of the United States before, and the decision would certainly not be without its sacrifices, especially for their own children. But even as the Jacobsons sold their house, placed their furniture in storage, and bought one-way tickets to Thailand, they remained determined all the while to see their vision come to fruition.

AS THE JACOBSON children settled into a school for missionary kids in Chiang Mai, one of the first things Jim and Karen did when they arrived in Thailand was to visit the construction site.

Trash lay strewn around the perimeter of the building, and unsightly vegetation crawled up the partially constructed walls. As they stepped inside, they were dismayed to see splashes of paint and concrete across the ceramic floor tiles; the workers had apparently begun to lay the flooring before moving on to the tasks of painting and mixing cement. As they took it all in, one dawning realization sank heavily into their minds: there was a lot of work to be done.

But if the project was ever to be finished, more manpower would definitely be needed, and Jim began driving around to local job sites in search of able-bodied men. With the help of his translator, he unabashedly asked the workers how much they were getting paid, then offered top dollar in exchange for their agreement to drop what they were doing and come work for him instead. After hours of dogged recruiting, Jim finally organized a labor party that would assist with all aspects of the school's construction, everything from installing electrical systems to flooring and painting.

The work was finally picking up, but Jim soon found that, on any given day, he still faced a number of challenges at the construction site. As an American familiar with the daily juggling act of multitasking, he was quietly frustrated by the natives' strange, archaic work methods. When he caught several workers pouring paint onto the floor, he patiently demonstrated how to use paint trays and rollers. And on several occasions, when many of the Buddhist workers stopped construction out of fear of being attacked by evil spirits due to a bout of "bad luck," Jim tolerantly complied with their request to offer sacrificial chickens to the spirits before the work continued.

But incidents with the construction workers weren't the only surprises Jim had to deal with. While helping to install flooring one afternoon, he was interrupted from his work by the sound of excited shouting outside. Wondering with mild annoyance what could possibly be the matter now, he looked out a nearby window to see a crowd of workers, yelling in Burmese and pointing frantically behind him. As Jim turned around, he caught sight of a Siamese cobra next to him, poised and ready to strike. With a rush of terrified adrenaline, he leapt up onto the window frame as the workers rushed in and killed the snake with a long, heavy stick. It would be the first of many cobras they would have to kill while working on the property.

He traveled from his temporary home in Chiang Mai to Mae Sot on a weekly basis to oversee the construction, intermittently running errands to various stores to purchase many of the necessary supplies himself. Most of his time, however, was spent alongside his workers, hammering, painting, and laying tile in the building that was, at long last, beginning to show signs of promise. With the occasional sound of distant gunshots across the border, Jim labored tirelessly on the dream that God was finally bringing together, one brick at a time.

Intercession for the Saints

As you start meeting people in the persecuted church, it becomes real to you, and then you start to get a passion for it. And you realize that these are our brothers and sisters in Christ, and we belong to the same family.

Going places where there's no sanitation, where people have no homes, at first it's very overwhelming. It can consume you, so you can't deal with things. But then you come to a point where you just have to give it over to God. He knows, so that's how I handle these things.

I've never been angry or questioned God, but I've just come to realize how fortunate I am to be born in America, and that I'm an American citizen. My work has given me much more of a passion for America and to preserve our freedom, because America does so much to help other countries, and it's a great thing.

Jim Jacobson

Nam Thuam, Laos
March, 2004

THE GOVERNMENT AGENTS appeared on the doorsteps of 35 families one morning, with an ultimatum that would endure a supreme test of wills: if the families did not renounce their Christian faith, the agents would move into their homes until they did. What was more, each household would have to pay for the agent's living expenses until every family member had either denied their Christianity or moved out of the village.

No one renounced their faith, and not a single bag was packed.

The agents forced their way into the families' homes, where their presence soon overshadowed every aspect of their lives. The existence of the unwelcome houseguests meant that the Christians were unable to pray, read the Bible, or worship together—except, of course, when they dared to do it in secret.

One of the world's few remaining Communist states, Laos was a country where its longstanding campaign to eradicate any traces of Christianity had escalated in recent years. Buddhism was the nation's dominant force, with Animism coming behind it at a close second—but according to the government, Christian teachings signified great disloyalty to the Communist Party, and had to be severely restricted at all costs. Although there were a few government-approved churches, most Christians in Laos were forced to secretly worship in illegal house churches. And anyone, including a foreigner, who was caught proselytizing or attempting to distribute Christian material of any sort would surely face arrest.

142

The agents' intrusion into the believers' homes was the kind of everyday thing that occurred in Laos—the government pressured its Christian citizens, and they, in turn, endured the arrests, intimidation and harassment in quiet helplessness. After years of living under the ruthless authorities who seemed bent on denying them any sort of religious rights, there wasn't much else to do, after all. Many of them had been arrested and placed in forced labor camps, often working in rice fields for months at a time without pay. As the government used any and all excuses to keep the Christian population under its control, others were imprisoned after being falsely accused of one crime or another.

Jim had personally documented the stories of many persecuted Christians during his trips to Laos, and he wasn't content to stand idly by while they suffered. Through a series of petitions, press releases, and articles in the CFI newsletter, he urged both American citizens and the United States government to take a stand for Christians in Laos, as well as urging the country's own government to end the forced renunciations, confiscation of Bibles, destruction of churches, and the release of its Christian prisoners.

He joined indigenous workers to help deliver medicine and dental care in remote villages, even accepting an invitation to set up a makeshift hospital in a local Buddhist temple. It was a valuable opportunity to demonstrate the love of Christ to the many lost souls who suddenly appeared in the crowd, and the medical team provided care for a number of Buddhist patients as well as Christians during the visit. Before he left, Jim prayed for everyone in the village, explaining to those who regarded him so curiously that he and his workers were there because they were helping their brothers and sisters in Christ. But just as importantly, they were also willing to help individuals and families who did not yet know Jesus, the Savior who had died for each and every one of them, even while they were still sinners.

FROM HIS TEMPORARY home in Chiang Mai, Thailand, Jim continued overseeing the construction of the vocational school in Mae Sot, even as he spent months making several trips to neighboring Laos.

The school was, at long last, nearing completion, and a small group of college-aged refugee students had already spent a brief stint at the school before returning to the camps. With the first set of volunteer teachers in place, Jim and Karen were excited to see the school reach the final stages of transition. Things had fallen into place with amazing precision, and not just with the overall construction process. With the help of several Christian attorneys Jim and Karen had met during their stay in Thailand, CFI not only obtained the legal status necessary to run the school, but were granted work permits for its staff.

It was as if God Himself had opened the doors of the CFI Vocational School.

The first group of junior and senior high school students arrived in May of 2004. In a flurry of excitement and apprehension, nearly two dozen teenage refugees boarded a van for Mae Sot, wondering about the new adventure that would begin to reshape their lives. As they traveled along winding roads to reach their destination, even a bout with carsickness would only temporarily dampen their anticipation.

The learning process began even before they set foot in a classroom. As the children settled into the school's dormitories, they were trained in the simplest routines of modern, everyday living—sleeping in a bed, how to use showers and toilets, or even using a light switch. And yet, with the instruction most of them had already received in CFI-sponsored orphanages, they were more prepared for the endeavor than many other kids their age.

Just a few weeks after the school's official opening, Karen packed up the Jacobson children and returned to the United States, while Jim remained in Thailand for several more weeks to tie up loose ends. He was grateful that the project was finally complete, and while the past year had certainly been remarkable, he was glad to go home to the familiar surroundings of Virginia.

But he would return to the school as often as possible on his trips, amazed at how quickly the children were learning and growing as the months wore on. He loved talking with them, spending time with them, challenging them to games of dodge ball in the school's front yard, and enjoying the fact that the children looked forward to each one of his visits just as much as he did. With hopeful prayer, they would all go on to lead better lives once their time at the school came to an end. There had been a variety of challenges to overcome throughout the entire process, but to Jim, every single moment had been worth the effort.

Without question, he would do it all again if he had to.

PETER KHALEQUE HAD no idea of the trouble that awaited him the day he shared his Christian faith with a colleague in his homeland of Bangladesh.

At first, the man he'd spoken to was receptive to the Gospel, even claiming to accept Jesus Christ as his newfound Savior. But when the man's wife learned about his conversion, and how Peter, the former police officer turned Christian pastor, had had a hand in the unspeakable act, legal charges were promptly filed against him.

Peter feared for the safety of his 12-year-old daughter as he was arrested and sent to prison. Without his protection, abduction, rape, and forced conversion to Islam were all very possible scenarios for his young child. The details surrounding his case quickly escalated into false charges of beatings and bodily injury against the wife of the man with whom he'd so innocently shared his faith, until one terrible realization began to dominate Peter's thoughts: somewhere, somehow, he'd lost any sense of basic human rights.

Eventually, the colleague renounced his Christianity and dropped the false charges against Peter, but not before the stress of the entire ordeal had driven him to a near mental and physical breakdown. Although the lawsuit had been dropped, he knew the authorities were still actively pursuing his case, determined to find some other way to return him to prison—he was a Christian, after all, and prison was where Christians belonged in Bangladesh. He was also still concerned for the safety of his daughter, who was the subject of ominous phone calls he'd been receiving from strangers who were threatening to kidnap her.

His life, it seemed, had become one unending nightmare—and all because, in a moment of compassion, he'd dared to reach out to another soul to share the good news about Jesus Christ.

AS PETER WAS enduring his own trials, two Christian women were also in the fight of their lives.

Shahanaz Alam and Kumekume Roy, both converts from Islam, lived in the constant fear and anxiety that had become familiar to other Bangladeshi Christians. In an ongoing quest to dodge the menacing harassment and death threats, Shahanaz spent her days moving secretly from place to place, even as her faith grew and she shared the Gospel with anyone who would listen. For Kumekume, the fear was even more deeply rooted — she had already once been abducted, beaten, and raped by a Muslim man who refused to accept her conversion. If she was captured again, she could very well be killed. The situation was all too common in Bangladesh — Christian women suffered gross mistreatment, often dragged back into the Islamic culture by forced marriage, without any type of governing authority doing anything about it.

As the women finally found refuge in a CFI safe house, Jim carefully documented their testimonies, as well as the testimony of Peter Khaleque, and contacted several members of the U.S. Congress, the State Department, and even attorneys in Bangladesh with their stories. He was deeply concerned about the country's growing persecution of Muslim converts to Christianity, and had become intensely involved in an asylum assistance mission that provided safe houses, legal and political advocacy, transportation, food and medicine for believers on the run.

In Bangladesh, Christian converts often lost everything — their jobs, homes, possessions, and even their families — because of their decision to follow Jesus Christ, and the disabled were among those especially hurt by severe persecution. With practically no government services available to rely on for assistance, many minority Christians resorted to a life of harsh poverty, even begging in the streets. As CFI developed its outreach ministry among a strong network of indigenous workers, its efforts quickly took root in the country. But although the organization's supply of food, clothing and even Braille Bibles for the blind were making a difference in the lives of many suffering believers, the needs of the persecuted church in Bangladesh remained sadly overwhelming.

As more countries became increasingly dangerous places for Christians to live in or even visit, Jim's personal safety, and that of his workers, had become more of a concern than ever. He traveled to Tongi, Bangladesh in the winter of 2004, with plans to attend a secret baptism for dozens of new Christian converts. The event was to be held during *Biswa Ijtema*, a three-day Muslim celebration that culminated in a final day of prayer. While Muslims from around the world were busy taking part in one of their largest religious gatherings, CFI workers hoped to enjoy their own ceremony in a temporary house church just outside Tongi. The plan was to dismiss the baptismal service at the conclusion of the Muslim holiday, with enough time to allow the new converts to quietly disappear to places of relative safety.

But as it turned out, danger was already looming nearby. Even before the baptismal ceremony could begin, CFI workers discovered that Muslim extremists, reinvigorated by the massive, three-day gathering in the streets of Tongi, were secretly planning to strike the infidels, killing not only apostate Christians but those who proselytized them. With strong indications that the location of the scheduled baptism had been discovered by the extremists, plans for the meeting were quickly abandoned. Jim, his co-workers, and the new converts all scattered to various locations throughout the region, vowing to reschedule the ceremony once things were safer.

By God's grace, everyone narrowly escaped what could have been a violent disaster. Nevertheless, the incident was one more reminder that, as always, God was holding a guiding hand not only on Christian Freedom International, but on the very life of its president.

INDONESIA WAS ANOTHER Muslim country within the reach of CFI's humanitarian arm.

The organization had been providing aid to the troubled region for years, after a series of violent attacks against Christians in the Spice Islands in 2002, and the devastating tsunami that destroyed nearly everything in its path on Nias Island in December 2004. Although Muslims and Christians had historically co-existed in Indonesia with a minimal amount of conflict, the country's growing number of radical Muslims was beginning to have an influence on local and national government.

The result was increasing hostility, harassment, and even murder of Christians, all while authorities looked the other way. True to form, Jim spent his visits documenting the large number of churches that had been forcibly closed by Muslim authorities, and subsequently urged CFI supporters to join a movement pressuring Indonesia's government to intervene in the rising antagonism towards its own Christian citizens.

With the help of a local pastor, he paid a visit to three Christian women who were serving a lengthy prison sentence in Indramayu in the fall of 2005. Determined to capture their story, Jim remained insistent on taking both his camera and laptop computer into the visitor's area, despite protests from prison officials.

Dr. Rebekka Zakaria, Eti Pangesti, and Ratna Bangun had run a Sunday School program in their church, and allowed the admission of several Muslim children into the school only after obtaining verbal consent from the students' guardians. But when a local Islamic group brought charges against them for the crime of attempting to "coerce" the children into changing their religion, the women were quickly arrested.

At the time of Jim's visit, they had served 140 days of their three-year sentence.

Conditions in the prison were cramped at best, with eight women forced to share one small, dirty cell. They all slept together on top of hard, wooden platforms, without even the smallest comfort of blankets or sheets. When there was a need to use the cell's toilet, the prison guards had to be bribed to turn on the water. Meals often consisted of one egg-sized lump of a rice and soybean mixture, which was usually covered with ants.

Although the women sorely missed their families and dreamed constantly about going home, daily sessions of prayer and Bible reading were helping them through the ordeal. With the kind of loving forgiveness that only true Christianity could bring, they harbored no resentment against the people who were responsible for their imprisonment. Instead, they chose to trust in a God who faithfully brought them new joy and peace each day, despite their dismal circumstances.

The women were excited at Jim's interest in their case, and Jim promised to rally as much support for them as possible. But if nothing else, they wanted to be sure the American Christian took one thing with him before he left: a promise to pray. No Christian was safe in Indonesia, and although they wanted the world to know about their situation, what they really needed was the prayerful support of as many other believers as possible. Please pray for us, Rebekka pleaded with Jim from the stifling confines of her prison world.

Please, pray...

A Future and a Hope

Only in America can something like this happen, where you can take some kid from the Midwest like me who shouldn't be doing what I do now, and make it a story. But that's the story of Christianity. When you really surrender your life to Jesus Christ, you just never know what you're going to do or where you're going to end up, and that's the exciting and liberating thing about Christianity.

Without that, I wouldn't be anything — none of us would be anything.

Jim Jacobson

Sault Ste. Marie, Michigan
1988

THE CHRISTIANS OF Sault Ste. Marie were praying — again.

The Sensual Arts Adult Bookstore on Ashmun Street had been a disturbing presence in the community for months, and finally, local believers felt compelled to fall on their knees and pray about the situation.

Rich in history as well as natural beauty, Sault Ste. Marie was the oldest city in Michigan, and one of the oldest cities in the United States. The Soo Locks, one of the busiest maritime passageways in the world and located within the city's borders, was a strong tourist attraction, among others, that drew thousands of visitors to the region each year. But despite its strategic location in the Midwest and its close proximity to Canada, the city had spent years struggling through a sluggish economy before things finally began to pick up.

And then came the bookstore.

It was a most unwelcome establishment, in an even more undesirable industry, that seemed to be the bane of the entire community. And yet somehow, the store defiantly remained in the old building on Ashmun Street, in a location where tourists had to directly pass through in order to get to the Locks.

Determined to see the business fold, local church congregations made a crucial decision: they would pray. Not only would they pray that the bookstore would close its doors forever, but they would also pray that, someday, a strong, Christian-owned business or organization would rise up in its place.

The believers prayed over the building on Ashmun Street day in and day out, always with faithful determination. They had no idea when their petitions would finally be answered, but what they *did* know was that the Sensual Arts Adult Bookstore should have no place in their beloved town of Sault Ste. Marie.

AFTER YEARS OF hard work, Jim was more than pleased with Christian Freedom International's progress as an organization, as well as its ministry to the persecuted church.

He had a small but reliable staff helping to run the home office in Virginia, and several indigenous workers overseas that supervised programs in countries such as Thailand and Bangladesh. And although CFI could have always used more funds, the donations faithfully supplied by thousands of American supporters over the years had helped to provide more food, medicine, clothing and Bibles, and build more schools, orphanages and hospitals for suffering Christians than he ever thought possible.

But despite CFI's success, there were still a few things bothering Jim.

By early 2007, the U.S. resettlement process that would finally begin to open the door to freedom for thousands of Karen refugees was underway. While Jim was elated at the thought that many suffering Karen would finally be able to live and worship freely in the United States, the fate of five Karen siblings was burdening his heart. He'd made a solemn promise to their mother, before her recent death in a refugee camp, that he would always look out for her two sons and three young daughters. He hadn't been quite sure what he'd meant by the promise at the time, but as the children prepared to resettle in the United States, Jim and Karen began to consider adopting the now orphaned family.

There was just one problem — according to all official policies, adoption of refugee children was impossible. The widespread instability of Burma's refugee situation had rendered a unanimous decision from the United Nations, the U.S. State Department, and the Department of Health and Human Services: because no one could truly guarantee the existence — or nonexistence — of parents or other family members, adoption of refugee orphans was out of the question.

It was an answer that Jim chose not to accept. For as long as he could remember, it had been part of his nature to find a way to make something happen whenever he'd been told that it was otherwise impossible. What mattered most to him now was the fact that a young family was in dire need of help, and against all odds, he was determined to make them a part of his own family forever.

There was another problem that had been on Jim's mind — for even longer, in fact, than the issues surrounding the refugee resettlement. Ever since CFI had become an entity apart from Christian Solidarity International, the organization had relocated over six times in 12 years, including its move from Washington, D.C., where the cost of rent for one small office had simply been too expensive to afford. CFI's relocation from Washington to Virginia had been followed by a series of subsequent moves within the Shenandoah Valley area, always in search of an ideal building that would not only provide office space, but an adequate warehouse facility in which to store the growing inventory of microenterprise products.

To Jim, CFI's "nomad" lifestyle was simply unacceptable. Almost since the day he assumed leadership, it had been his dream to stabilize the organization with permanent headquarters, to set up a place where CFI would take root and continue to flourish even long after he was gone.

He'd also been considering the establishment of a museum dedicated to the persecuted church, another project that would require a much larger facility. After months of diligent research, Jim had come to the conclusion that no such museum existed in any known part of the country, or even the world. The plan for the museum was to design a self-guided tour through a variety of visual displays, all discussing the exact nature, statistics, and countries known for Christian persecution, as well as a gift shop that would include the sale of micro-enterprise handcrafts. Just as the Holocaust Museum memorialized the atrocities committed during World War II, Jim was determined to see his vision for what he so aptly called "The Center for Religious Freedom" someday come to pass.

But as his search for affordable commercial real estate failed to uncover any leads, his options for purchasing a new building in Virginia began to seem dismal. Even renovating an existing building would cost the organization far more than what it could afford, and unless a generous benefactor suddenly stepped out of the shadows, CFI had only the financial support of its donor base to rely on.

After exhausting what seemed to be all other options, Jim and Karen finally began discussing the possibility of relocating to another state. With all the recent advances in technology, there was certainly no reason why the organization had to stay in Virginia—the important thing was to find a location where they would not only be able to reduce their expenses, and ultimately increase the amount of funds applied to CFI programs, but a place where everyone could comfortably relocate. For days, Jim searched through an unending assortment of commercial properties on the Internet, everywhere from Alabama to New Hampshire, until a search in Michigan resulted in a list of several properties that finally seemed promising.

Jim had never considered the possibility of returning to his home state of Michigan, nor did he possess any real desire to do so. But in all fairness, the opportunities there seemed too ideal to ignore, or at least not to investigate. Real estate prices had been dropping sharply in the state, and he had his sights on one building in particular in the historic town of Sault Ste. Marie. Armed with their list of properties, he and Karen flew out to Traverse City, Michigan to begin the search, ultimately taking the three-hour drive to Sault Ste. Marie.

Their efforts would not be in vain. Although they finally decided against submitting an offer on the building Jim had found in Sault Ste. Marie—which, in fact, turned out to be a little too big for CFI's needs, and would have required too many expensive renovations—another opportunity in the city would quickly present itself. There was a building that housed an adult bookstore downtown, someone helpfully informed Jim. The building had once been for sale, and although it was no longer on the market, perhaps the owners would still be willing to consider an offer.

After one look at the property, the possibility did, indeed, seem to be one worth pursuing. The three-story, 7,600 square foot facility held enough space to accommodate both CFI's current and future needs, and Sault Ste. Marie was in fact an ideal town in which to relocate. The building's highly visible location in the downtown area would also mean more exposure to the general public, a factor that would be especially helpful for microenterprise sales. The entire building would need to be renovated, and the owner's asking price was slightly higher than other comparable properties on the market, but as long as they were moving into the area, Jim had resolutely decided that, if there was anything he could do about it, he wanted to remove the adult bookstore from the building — and the community — for good.

The offer to purchase was accepted, the paperwork was signed, and it was just a matter of time before the decision became official: Christian Freedom International was moving one last, final time to Michigan — into the very building on Ashmun Street that Sault Ste. Marie Christians had been praying over for two decades.

IT DIDN'T TAKE long for Betsy Demaray's request to the congregation of Central Methodist Church and the Sault Ste. Marie Rotary Club to spread throughout the community.

With the help of a humanitarian organization called Christian Freedom International, she announced, a refugee family from Burma would soon be moving into the area. Mercy Htoo, a teenage girl who'd once been a resident of a CFI orphanage in Thailand, had recently come to America with her family — her parents, two sisters and their husbands, and several nieces and nephews — and would be relocating to Michigan from their temporary home in Fort Wayne, Indiana the week after Thanksgiving. A new home had already been secured for them in Sault Ste. Marie, but a ton of renovation work was needed in the house. If anyone was willing and able to help with the repairs, their donation of time and labor would be greatly appreciated.

The response to Betsy's call for help would astonish Jim and Karen. Betsy was their realtor and a lifelong resident of Sault Ste. Marie, and in the short amount of time since they had moved to Michigan, had also become the Jacobsons' good friend. Jim had spent weeks working on the details of the Htoo family's relocation from Indiana, and with Betsy's help, had found an inexpensive home, complete with a rent to own option, that would suit the family's needs.

The Jacobsons had arrived at the vacant property the weekend before Thanksgiving, and were quickly overwhelmed by what they saw inside. The small house was cluttered with trash, smelled pungently of pet odors, and nearly everything was in need of repair. With the help of Karen's father, who had flown out to Michigan to visit, Jim began tearing up linoleum from the kitchen floor, only to discover layers of mold on the plywood underneath. The dilemma was obvious — they would not be able to clean and restore the house by themselves before the Htoo family's arrival. They would need as much help as they could possibly get.

They returned to the house the morning after Thanksgiving, pleasantly surprised to find Betsy and her husband already on the scene and ready to work. Other volunteers soon began to arrive, and throughout the course of the day pitched in to clean, paint, install linoleum, fix broken windows, replace carpeting, repair electrical and plumbing systems, and haul over two tons of debris to the local dump.

It was the kind of dedicated, heartfelt assistance that Jim and Karen had already become familiar with in the small town of Sault Ste. Marie. Since their own move to the area just a couple of months earlier, and as they worked on renovations to the new CFI building on Ashmun Street, they had been standing in a floodgate of support from a community that seemed to care about CFI's mission to the persecuted church just as much as they cared for the Jacobsons themselves. Now, they were surrounded by over 30 of their neighbors, all who had so willingly come together on behalf of a family from another country they'd never even met.

Word about the Htoo family's impending arrival continued to spread, and more help continued to arrive over the following days. As repairs to the house were finally completed, furniture, household items, toys and clothing were donated for the family, as well as gift cards to various supermarkets and department stores. And before they had even set foot in Michigan, local businesses already had jobs lined up for the refugees.

Accompanied by his nephew, Ben, Jim set out on the seven-hour drive to Indiana to retrieve the family, while more volunteers helped Karen with a final round of cleaning and preparation in the new house. Amid the bitter cold of a Michigan snowstorm, Jim escorted the Htoo family to Sault Ste. Marie on November 30, 2007 — into a welcoming community, a warm, inviting home, and the promise of a new life.

The excitement was evident on the refugees' faces from the moment they arrived in Michigan. They were in completely unfamiliar surroundings, and they had just stepped into the coldest, harshest weather they had ever experienced, but for the moment, they were grateful just to be *free*. For once in their lives, they were free to live, to work and provide for their family, to worship their God, and to dream about all the wonderful things to come. At long last, the chains of persecution had finally been broken, and with the help of their Christian brethren, they knew that, together, they would overcome whatever challenges came their way.

AS THE DUST began to settle in the wake of CFI's move to Michigan, one more window of opportunity was opening for Jim and Karen Jacobson.

After months of persistence, adoption plans for the refugee children Jim had been so determined to help were finally coming together. The family, headed by their 25-year-old brother and his 18-year-old wife, had been living in Richmond, Virginia since their move to the United States in September 2007. But despite the support they'd been receiving from the U.S. refugee re-settlement agency and a nearby church congregation, it was clear from Jim's visits to the family that they were still in great need of help. Although their hands were already full with their own four growing children, Jim and Karen had long since been reassured that adoption was, indeed, the best thing for the orphans from Burma.

Jim had been working with the resettlement agency in Virginia to iron out the lengthy details surrounding the adoption, and once again, it was a process that God seemed to be orchestrating for the Jacobsons. Htoo Eh Paw, 18 and the second oldest child in the family, would travel to Michigan with his younger sisters, 14-year-old Ku Taw Paw, 10-year-old Sa Gla Lay, and 8-year-old Say Lay Paw, as soon as they received word that it would be just a matter of time before they officially became members of the Jacobson family. Jim had also been working on relocation plans for their oldest brother and his wife, so the entire family would be able to travel to Michigan together.

Like the Htoo family, the children were over-whelmingly grateful for the exciting prospects that awaited them. They had been displaced from their homeland, languishing in the dismal surroundings of refugee camps, and had lived in the haunting shadows of fear, desperation, and persecution long enough— now, it was time for new beginnings. Through the love and devotion of a man named Jim Jacobson, God had

reached down, touched them in the midst of their suffering, and given them the kind of hope and a future
that, until now, had only been a distant dream.

For every Christian that managed to find refuge in
the United States, hundreds more would continue to
take their places in the fiery furnace of persecution –
and not just in Burma. For those fellow believers still
living in oppression, they could only pray and trust
God that all things would, indeed, be made right in the
end – if not in this life, then most certainly in the next.

Until then, Christian Freedom International would
be there.

*"For I know the thoughts that I think toward you, says
the LORD, thoughts of peace and not of evil, to give you a
future and a hope."*

Jeremiah 29:11

Index

Christian Freedom International (CFI) is a 501(c)(3) nonprofit organization that assists those who are persecuted for their faith in Jesus Christ.

For more information about CFI's mission, or to learn more about the persecuted church, contact CFI at:

Christian Freedom International
P.O. Box 560
Sault Ste. Marie, MI 49783
1-800-323-CARE
www.christianfreedom.com

Breinigsville, PA USA
28 September 2010
246243BV00002B/1/P